MORE ONE LINERS JOKES & GAGS

COMPILED BY
GRANT TUCKER

The Robson Press

First published in Great Britain in 2013 by
The Robson Press (an imprint of Biteback Publishing Ltd)
Westminster Tower
3 Albert Embankment
London SE1 7SP

ISBN 978-1-84954-619-5

10 9 8 7 6 5 4 3 2 1

A CIP catalogue record for this book is available from the British Library.

Set in Sabon

Printed and bound in Great Britain by
CPI Group (UK) Ltd, Croydon CR0 4YY

INTRODUCTION

My first compilation of *5,000 Great One-Liners* was, I felt, a fitting tribute to a great, comedic art form. It was said to have 'all the quips, zingers, puns and wise-cracks you'll ever need', but I've changed my mind about that. You can't have too many of these; you really can't.

If you got through *5,000 Great One-Liners* and felt gutted to have reached the end, then *More One-Liners, Jokes and Gags* is the book for you. And it's for every-one else, too. Because who doesn't love a good laugh? According to the internet (my source for all things both humorous and informative), laughter really is the best medicine. It relieves physical stress by relaxing the body, it boosts the immune system, it causes the release of endorphins and it protects you against heart attacks by improving blood flow. So there! This book isn't just good fun, it's also the healthy choice when it comes to reading material. And laughter is infectious, so you can pass it on, too.

With *More One-Liners, Jokes and Gags* I have paid homage to the immortal one-liner once again, but I've also gone even further and provided some side-splitting, eye-watering, belly-aching, face-cracking longer jokes for your enjoyment. Whether in a pub or on a toilet I'm sure these jokes will put a smile on your face.

Now, I would like to thank a few people who have put a smile on my face, and yes, it is usually when I'm in a pub. Namely my dad, Carl Tucker, who is always the first to crack a joke in any situation; my friend Holly Smith: all I need to do is look at her and she can make me laugh; my friends Huw Anslow and Dan Groves, who have the ability to turn the most serious moments into a joke; my friends Alex Davies and Abbie Thomas, who stopped maturing at the age of thirteen; and my cousin Jamie Tucker, who still laughs at my jokes from the first book. Iain Dale and Jeremy Robson, my publishers, also deserve a special mention.

Finally, I would like to thank my long-suffering editor Olivia Beattie for her patience during this mammoth project. I've brought a whole new meaning to the word 'deadline' and often left her pulling her hair out. But I am very grateful to her for making this book what it is today.

I do hope that this book gives you as much fun and laughter as it gave me when compiling it.

Grant Tucker
London, October 2013

THE JOKES

Went to the corner shop – bought four corners.

Why did a boy throw a clock out the window? To see time fly.

My teenage son threw the chemistry set I bought him onto the floor. If he thinks he's going to get a reaction that way, he's got a lot to learn.

Did you hear about the old chameleon that couldn't change colour? He had a reptile dysfunction.

Your momma's so fat that she should probably be worried about the increased risk of cardiovascular disease.

What do you call a deer with no eyes? No eye deer.

What do you call a deer with no eyes and no legs? Still no eye deer.

An autobiography is a book that reveals nothing bad about its writer except his memory.

Whenever I write a letter to someone, I add a footnote briefly explaining Ohm's law. It's my P.S. de resistance.

Why did the banana go to the hospital? Because he wasn't peeling well.

If procrastination was an Olympic sport, I'd compete in it later.

My girlfriend really bugged me last night. The perils of dating a spy.

I've bought a Samsung S4 and iPhone 5. Hopefully between them both I will have enough battery power to see me through my three-hour train journey.

I've invented a golf ball that automatically goes in the hole if it comes within a foot. Just don't carry them in your back pocket.

Two mysterious people live in my house. Somebody and Nobody. Somebody did it and Nobody knows who.

They say counting sheep will send you to sleep, but forty-seven lambs just walked into my front room and I've never been wider awake.

If someone asks you about a musical you haven't seen, fake it by saying, 'I love that part near the end when they all sing together.'

Most CVs are just neatly presented suicide notes.

I'm counting on you, fingers.

So I said, 'Do you want a game of darts?' He said, 'OK then.' I said, 'Nearest to bull starts.' He said, 'Baa.' I said, 'Moo.' He said, 'You're closest.'

You can't divorce yourself from reality if you were never married to it in the first place.

People tell me how hard it is to stop smoking; I think it's about as hard as it is to start flossing.

What's small and red and whispers? A hoarse radish.

Just had a rant in which I said I hope the entire world explodes tomorrow. Probably went too far. Sorry for including you all.

Starting to think no one's *ever* going to make a desperate grab for my ankle as I leave a room.

What do you call a handcuffed man? Trustworthy.

From the moment our eyes first met, I knew I would spend the rest of my life avoiding you.

What is The Fonz's blood type? AAAAAAAAAAAA.

There's a lot to be said for being a man of few words.

What do you call a boy named Lee that no one talks to? Lonely.

I always mean what I say … I just don't always mean to say it out loud.

Don't steal. That's the government's job.

I went out last Friday and got drunk out of my mind. I woke up next to this sweaty bird who was snoring, grunting and farting. I thought, thank God for that, I made it home!

I saw a sign on a Scottish golf course once. It said, 'Members will please refrain from picking up lost balls until they have stopped rolling.'

Why did the snowman take his pants off? He heard the snow blower was coming.

I took my wife to the pictures today. And pointed out the layer of dust on each one.

My favourite time of self-reflection is when the mirrors are fogged after a shower.

Alcoholism is a disease, but it's the only one you can get yelled at for having.

What did the hurricane say to the coconut palm tree? 'Hold on to your nuts, this is no ordinary blow job!'

How does the ocean say hello? It waves.

I live in a two-storey house. One of them is 'it's always your fault' and the other one is 'because I said so'.

Round and round the garden like a teddy bear? You really need to stop drinking.

'You're not the person I fell in love with!' is a fun thing to say to anyone who isn't the person you fell in love with.

The barman says, 'We don't serve faster-than-light particles here.' A tachyon enters a bar.

'I feel like a million bucks.' – Nymphomaniac deer.

Why was six afraid of seven? Because seven was a six offender.

The inventor of the doorbell did not own a chihuahua.

A one-man band is a multiple personality disorder in musical form.

The first step is admitting that the other person is the one with the problem.

Three people were in a boat. They all fell off. Only two people ended up with wet hair. Why didn't the other person's hair get wet? Because he was bald.

I got in touch with my inner self today. That's the last time I buy Tesco Value toilet roll.

I was thrown out of university because they caught me cheating on my metaphysics exam. I looked within the soul of the boy sitting next to me.

Pretend you're a millionaire whale by spraying champagne through the sunroof of a limousine.

If I murdered someone and put real effort into covering my tracks, there's absolutely no way I'd not tell detectives exactly how I did it.

How does the man on the moon cut his hair? Eclipse it.

Did you hear about the guy who died of a Viagra overdose? They couldn't close his casket.

I always say, follow your dreams. Except for that one where you're naked at work.

How does a Jewish mother change a light bulb? 'No, that's all right. I'll just sit here in the dark.'

If my iPod doesn't work in the next few minutes, I'm throwing it in the river. It can either sync or swim.

Panic attack: When you don't feel your phone in your pocket.

'Stop blaming me for everything!' – The Boogie.

I was voted the 'worst employee in the nursing home' recently. I don't care.

I went to the local video shop and I said, 'Can I take out *The Elephant Man*?' He said, 'He's not your type.' I said, 'Can I borrow *Batman Forever*?' He said, 'No, you'll have to bring it back tomorrow.'

You can always tell a transvestite because they hang down from the ceiling, while transvesmites grow up from the floor.

Imagine not wanting a *Starlight Express*-themed funeral.

I'm pretty sure the word 'studying' was derived from the words 'students dying'.

Maybe my rap handle is 'Casual T'.

Why did the Dalai Lama visit Las Vegas? Tibet.

Seriously, is there anything worse than bumping into someone you know?

The condensed history of a divorce: I do. Ado. Adieu.

What do you call a deaf man with no limbs? Whatever you want.

The *Daily Mail* has left me slightly confused. Do millions of immigrants come to Britain to steal our jobs or claim our benefits?

The team I support because I liked their kit when I was four beat the team you support because they were good when you were six. Let's argue.

'Business is terrible, but let's keep things in perspective: nobody died.' – Bankrupt funeral director.

You must have been born on a motorway, because that's where most accidents happen.

What do you call a boomerang that won't come back? A stick.

It's very dangerous to wave to people you don't know because what if they don't have hands? They'll think you're cocky.

Police have warned that anyone reading *The Guardian* when it leaks British official secrets will be liable for prosecution. Estimates suggest that as many as ten people will be affected.

I think I speak for everyone when I say people who think they speak for everyone are idiots.

I was at a wedding the other day. It was so moving, even the cake was in tiers.

Where do generals keep their armies? Up their sleevies.

Why was the doctor so cross when he went on holiday? He had no patients.

What has two legs and is red all over? Half a dog.

If you lend someone money and you never see that person again, it was probably worth it.

Still haven't seen a squirrel that didn't look like he'd had far too much coffee.

For once in my life, I'd like to get up in the morning and be as excited about it as my dick is.

Ghetto translations: Shit just got real = The situation has escalated to the highest point of seriousness and is no longer a laughing matter.

I wouldn't trust my credit card with any of my friends yet I'll give it to just about any bartender.

So I rang up my local swimming baths. I said, 'Is that the local swimming baths?' He said, 'It depends where you're calling from.'

I told my wife I wanted breakfast in bed. She said I could go sleep in the kitchen.

How can I be sure I've succeeded if I can't remember what I was trying to do?

If this satsuma's a reliable guide, it would take me at least two weeks to undress a woman if my hands were cold.

Why didn't the skeleton cross the road? Because it had no guts.

Which type of boat has the most seamen on it? A tugboat.

What do you call a man with a seagull on his head? Cliff.

If you're stuck in a one-horse town you should steal the horse and ride out. They won't be able to catch you.

I don't drink to forget, I … what was I saying again?

I was hungover this morning. I phoned work and said to the boss, 'I'm afraid I won't be in today, my father had a massive heart attack and died last night.' 'That was your last chance, Dave,' he said, 'I'm taking the "and son" off the shop sign.'

A cement mixer collided with a prison van. Motorists are asked to be on the lookout for sixteen hardened criminals.

Seriously, can a man wearing pyjamas not buy wine at 9 a.m. without people assuming something is wrong?

Why did the tomato blush? Because he saw the salad dressing.

What doesn't kill you makes you stronger? Are you sure? I just ate my own bodyweight in ice cream and now I can't move.

Never be afraid to try something new. Remember, amateurs built the ark. Professionals built the *Titanic*.

Twitter is the only place where you're thrilled when a complete stranger starts following you.

Nothing sounds quite as sarcastic as a parrot being interrogated.

One of the World's Strongest Man events should be pulling apart two shopping carts that are stuck together.

Using a parsnip rather than a carrot will stop your snowman looking like someone who put fake tan on his nose then changed his mind.

How do they serve smart hamburgers? On honour rolls.

A zombie apocalypse and a machete would solve so many of my problems.

What do pimps and farmers have in common? They both need a hoe to stay in business.

When I was six, my dad threw me into the pool thinking I would instantly learn to swim. I probably would have if it had had water in it.

Putting spaghetti into boiling water is like taking dozens of strait-laced accountants and spiking their drinks.

Sometimes autocorrect can be your worst enema.

'Monday messes me up.' – Dynamo.

Just had sex even though I had a headache. Did you hear that, ladies? Nobody died…

What do you call a ninety-year-old man who can still masturbate? Miracle Whip.

I was at the circus and one of the clowns farted. It didn't half smell funny.

When I was on acid I would see things like beams of light, and I would hear things that sounded an awful lot like car horns.

What kind of driver has no arms or legs? A screwdriver.

Fun fact: I was at least twenty before I realised the Heimlich manoeuvre wasn't a notorious Nazi torture method.

We have nothing to fear except fear itself and toddlers asking 'Why?'

So this bloke says to me, 'Can I come in your house and talk about your carpets?' I thought, 'That's all I need, a Je-hoover's Witness.'

What has three letters and starts with gas? A car.

Onions make me sad. A lot of people don't realise that.

I'm a hard act to follow, because when I'm done, I take the microphone with me.

What do sea monsters eat for lunch? Fish and ships.

Cinderella is my favourite story about a wealthy foot fetishist who will only marry women with a very specific shoe size.

Strange that the more time you spend in the wilderness, the more you risk dying of exposure.

Made love to the wife last night just like they do in the movies. I was fast, she was furious.

My uncle died doing something he loved. He was lying in bed, completely ignoring my aunt yelling at him to wake up.

Two pieces of tarmac walk into a bar. They see this red bit of tarmac playing pool. The first bit of tarmac says to the second piece, 'Don't go near him.' The second piece says, 'Why?' The first piece of tarmac says, 'Because he's a cycle path.'

One day, a little boy wrote to Santa Claus, 'Please send me a sister.' Santa Claus wrote me back, 'OK, send me your mother.'

I've woken up looking like the exception that proves a particularly stupid rule.

Calendars? Their days are numbered.

When I was a kid my parents moved a lot, but I always found them.

I used to like the mirror that I had in 2002 much more than the one I have now.

Some guy knocked on my door today and said, 'I have a parcel for your next-door neighbour.' I said, 'You've got the wrong house then, mate.'

My wife started flashing her nipples trying to get into a club. I shouted, 'For God's sake, love, pull your skirt down!'

My CV is basically just a list of things I hate doing.

I accidentally dialled 999 from my mobile phone last night. So I set my house on fire so I wouldn't look stupid.

Apparently, California has the highest rates of adultery and depression. It's a sad state of affairs.

Don't think of people as touchy. Think of them as half-way to being touchy-feely.

Two muffins are in the oven. One says to the other, 'God, it's hot in here.' The other replies, 'Oh no ... It's a talking muffin.'

It's so ridiculous that bees fly into your house like it's perfectly normal, then behave like idiots when you put your face into their hive.

The worst thing about Mike Leigh's new massage parlour is that their idea of a happy ending is one where 'not that many people die'.

The Queen must be so upset that all the children she's visited in hospital don't return the favour.

Eating mints on a train is a good way to tell the person sitting next to you that you've not ruled out the possibility of kissing them.

What did the belly button say just before it left? I'm outtie here!

I really hope the girl sitting opposite's wearing false eyelashes and her head *isn't* being eaten by a pair of blue, glittery spiders.

Anything I can do, my wife can do bitter.

The man who invented the barbecue has died. The last thing he'd want is to be cremated.

When food falls on the floor, the little germs scream 'Let's get it!' while the mama germ says, 'No, we must wait five seconds.'

Going to get the word 'standards' printed on my underpants. Then I can raise them or lower them, depending on the quality of the women I meet.

Who was the world's first carpenter? Eve, because she made Adam's banana stand.

Eight out of ten experts agree that the other two are idiots who should stop being thought of as experts.

What is a baby's motto? If at first you don't succeed, cry, cry and cry again.

We breathe air, trees make air, homework kills trees. Therefore, homework kills us.

Give a man a fish, and he can eat for a day. But teach a man to fish, and he will bore you to death with fishing stories.

It's outrageous how many freelance contributors to the Bible are still awaiting royalties.

Pavlov is enjoying a pint in the pub. The phone rings. He jumps up and shouts, 'Hell, I forgot to feed the dog!'

Every Olympic event should include one average person competing, for reference.

I try to donate to charity, but they keep bringing my kids back.

I'm not a huge fan of biology, but there will always be a special place in my heart for pumping blood to organs and muscles.

Fool me once, shame on you. Fool me twice, shame on me. Fool me 2,591 times, you're my ex-girlfriend, who left because of my OCD.

Prison walls are never built to scale.

Why was the boy sitting on his watch? Because he wanted to be on time.

What do you call a man who pays for things? Bill.

A man walks into a doctor's surgery. He has a cucumber in his nose, a carrot in his left ear and a banana in his right ear. 'Ah! I can see what's the matter with you,' says the doctor. 'You're not eating properly.'

What did the blanket say when it fell off the bed? Oh sheet!

What does a man with two right feet wear to the beach? Flop-flops.

Bring a sense of magic and intrigue to your fruit machine addiction by calling it 'The Amazing Vanishing Coin Trick'.

I have recently downgraded my plans for this time next year from 'millionaire' to 'not homeless'.

What's worse than finding a horse's head on your pillow? Realising the horse is alive and well and how much did I drink last night?

My wife phoned me just before the show and said, 'I've got water in the carburettor.' I said, 'Where's the car?' She said, 'In the river.'

What is blue and goes ding dong? An Avon lady at the North Pole.

Managers: Some people need the carrot, others the stick. Play safe and give your staff carrot sticks.

That whole 'I'll scratch your back if you scratch mine' thing doesn't work so well with cats.

Fun fact: I have loyalty cards from seven different coffee shops.

Marriage is the most expensive way to get advice for nothing.

I'm always afraid my wife will leave me for a midget because he under stands.

I bought my wife a vibrator last month and it's already broken. But hey, that's the risk you take when you buy stuff at car boot sales.

Wait, there's nothing in this Air and Space Museum!

What did the bartender say when oxygen, hydrogen, sulphur, sodium, and phosphorus walked into his bar? OH SNaP!

Our ice-cream man was found lying on the floor of his van covered with hundreds and thousands. Police say that he topped himself.

I've just fixed the work radio that had been broken for months, my colleagues were ecstatic. You should have heard the reception I got.

'Baby, You Can Drive My Car' is my favourite song about irresponsible parenting.

Bob Marley explaining how and why he shot the sheriff shows just the sort of poor decision-making you'd associate with excessive drug use.

What kind of shoes do bananas make? Slippers.

I once dated a girl who wrote mystery novels, but it didn't last. Her hand jobs always ended with a surprise twist.

At work I realised that some ass was giving names to all of the food in the fridge. Today I had a tuna sandwich named 'Bob'.

I may not be the only egomaniac in the world, but I am the only one who matters.

Common sense is like deodorant: the people who need it most never use it.

If having dogs has taught me anything, it's how to eat biscuits very quietly.

Recreate the famous tracking shot from *Goodfellas* by walking all the way from one place to another without stopping.

'I am the love that dare not speak its name.' – Anonymous.

Which of these doesn't belong: lobster, crab, tuna, or a Chinese man run over by a bus? Tuna. All the others are crustaceans.

I'm going to purchase a dictionary, because after watching *Final Destination 5*, I clearly don't understand the meaning of the word 'final'.

'Tiniest planet ever discovered.' Are they sure it's not just really far away?

What nails do carpenters hate to hit? Fingernails.

It's raining men – hallelujah! No, wait: it's a group of estate agents doing a charity skydive. Run for the hills!

Breaking news: Police investigating burglary at actor Will Smith's home. I wonder if they'll find any fresh prints.

What did the clock do after it ate? It went back four seconds.

Sex is like playing bridge: if you don't have a good partner, you'd better have a good hand.

I've woken up looking like a tie you'd expect the wacky guy in Accounts to wear.

I broke into my neighbour's house and stole the keys to his Ferrari. I love keys.

My parents always told me I could be anyone I wanted and now I've been charged with identity theft. Parents cannot be trusted.

Every time I open my mouth, some idiot starts talking.

If you watch *Jaws* backwards, it's about a shark who throws up so many people they have to open a beach.

It was my son's birthday so I decided to take four of his friends to McDonald's and then bowling. They had a great time, he would've loved it.

Do I have insomnia or amnesia? I was up all night thinking about it, but I've forgotten which is which.

Why do birds suddenly appear every time you are near? Because I've hidden breadcrumbs in your pockets.

I really wish I knew who kicked the jack out from under the car I was working on. The suspension is killing me.

Douglas Engelbart, the inventor of the mouse, has died. What vision, to know we'd need one hand free on the computer.

What's green and flies as fast as a speeding bullet? Super Pickle!

That was actually really funny. But I don't like you. Therefore I shall not laugh.

If you're a beekeeper, always dress for the job you have, not the one you want.

I had my identity stolen during an identity crisis, so luckily they're only spending the money of the person I *thought* about becoming.

'There are plenty more fish in the sea' is a good thing to say to a child whose goldfish just died.

A bathroom tile salesman's pitch should be 'This tile will look great in the background of your Facebook pictures.'

Sometimes I drink my whisky neat. Other times I take my tie off and leave my shirt out.

I don't trust anything that can kill me, like wild animals or angry women.

Just explained Google images to my mum. 'Pick anything to search for,' I said. She replied, 'What about a nice cream pie?' 'Except that,' I said.

Why people say I'm ignorant, I'll never know.

What is the difference between a locomotive engineer and a teacher? One minds the train, one trains the mind.

Maybe your marbles don't want to be found.

I was in a restaurant with my girlfriend when I got down on one knee. She cried, 'I can't believe this is happening.' 'Shut up,' I said, 'my wife just walked in.'

Phone answering machine message: '... If you want to buy marijuana, press the hash key...'

I can't even imagine how sad I'll be if I ever find out that *Goldilocks and the Three Bears* isn't a true story.

Was your daddy a thief? Because if he was, I'm ending this conversation right now. Nobody wants a thief for a father-in-law.

What goes on and on and has an i in the middle? An onion.

I've lost my mind and I'm pretty sure my kids took it.

If the red house is on the left, the blue house is on the right, where is the White House? In Washington, DC.

My wife is going away for a weekend session with her gorgeous personal trainer. I find this very worrying. Why do I refer to him as gorgeous?

Shoepidity: Wearing ridiculously uncomfortable shoes just because they look good.

Behind every great man is a great woman. And behind them both is a queue of children looking forward to their inheritance.

I bought some HP sauce the other day. It's costing me 6p a month for the next two years.

Why doesn't a chicken wear pants? Because his pecker is on his head.

My life can be summed up as the end credits of *Saturday Night Live* where everyone's hugging and I'm the cameraman.

A lie is a very poor substitute for the truth, but it's the only one discovered so far.

Imagine wanting people to take you seriously when you're wearing a hat.

My train just approached the platform the same way I approach girls: stuttering along at the end of a queue, then breaking down completely.

'I hope you get better' is a fun thing to write in the Get Well Soon card of a colleague you genuinely feel should be better at their job.

Some of the children pushing ahead of me in the queue for this slide need to grow up.

If you flip through all of my Instagram pictures really fast, it's like watching a documentary on ageing.

Imagine finding a shoe in a phone box and not being furious that someone stole the rest of Superman's clothes.

I went on a blind date last night. 'I like men who are honest,' she said, 'what about you?' I said, 'I like women who can give good blow jobs.'

I hate when I leave the supermarket and can't find my car and panic, then find it and cry but it just sits there sulking like a child.

You never know a person until you walk in their shoes … or until you check their browser history.

History repeats itself, especially deleted internet history.

China has a population of a billion people. One billion. That means even if you're a one in a million kind of guy, there are still a thousand others exactly like you.

Why do chicken coops have two doors? Because if it had four doors it'd be a chicken sedan.

What does an angry pepper do? It gets jalapeño face.

I saw a fat person wearing a sweatshirt with 'Guess' on it. I said, 'Thyroid problem?'

Falling asleep during an interview is an excellent way to show you're calm under pressure.

She's so far out of my league she's playing for the other team.

My girlfriend asked me, 'Do you believe in love at first sight?' I said, 'At the first sight of what?'

What runs around a garden without moving? A fence.

Teacher: How old is your dad? Student: He is as old as I am. Teacher: How is it possible? Student: Because he became a dad only after I was born.

So I said to the taxi driver, 'King Arthur's Close.' He said, 'Don't worry, we'll lose him at the next set of lights.'

I speak four languages: English, profanity, sarcasm and real shit.

When I was born the doctor said to my mother, 'Congratulations you've just given birth to an 8lb ham.'

Google+ is the gym of social networking: we all join, but nobody actually uses it.

I wouldn't mind the couple who live above me having sex every night if a) they weren't mice, and b) they weren't doing it in *my* loft.

Whoever said there was money to be made from men wearing make-up, wigs and big red shoes was a right clown.

I'd talk to my wife more during sex if I were better at dialling the phone with one hand.

Why does it take 1 million sperm to fertilise one egg? They won't stop to ask directions.

It's a dog-eat-dog world out there. That's why I don't go out there. I stay in here where it's a man-eat-chocolate-cake world.

Pretend you're in a rom-com by asking an amusing gay man to be your best friend.

I don't hate people! At least 30 per cent of my best friends are people!

I asked the gym to teach me how to do the splits. They asked, 'How flexible are you?' I said, 'I can't make Tuesdays or Thursdays.'

My dad used to say 'always fight fire with fire', which is probably why he got thrown out of the fire brigade.

Massive sale on at Comet. Items are now only a bit more expensive than on Amazon.

What would happen if you cut off your left side? You'd be all right.

'Always leave them wanting more.' – Terrible parent.

A riddle, wrapped in a mystery, inside an enigma. Worst game of pass-the-parcel ever.

Throw lamps at people who need to lighten up.

I can be narcissistic, but luckily I make up for it by being incredibly handsome and charming.

I accidentally swallowed some Scrabble tiles. My next dump could spell disaster.

I was coming down into New York from Canada, driving through Customs, and the guy asked, 'Do you have any firearms with you?' I said, 'What do you need?'

I deserve a *much* greater sense of entitlement than I actually have.

Recreate the magic of Christmas by opening the windows of twenty-four houses and eating any chocolate you find inside.

When is it a good time to eat a window? When it's jammed.

A guy sticks his head in the barber shop and asks how long till he can get a haircut. The barber replies, 'About another half-inch.'

Jokes about German sausage are the wurst.

Every Tom, Dick or Harry's called Tom, Dick or Harry these days.

If you don't know which one of your friends isn't completely imaginary, it's you.

Why did the blonde starve to death? Her new phone came with a little packet in the box that said 'Do not eat.'

It's hard to write a good drinking song. I can never make it past the first few bars.

I'm making a TV show about hijacking a plane. We just shot the pilot.

I saw a sign on the bus the other day. It said 'Take the kids out for £1.' If you know of a cheaper hitman, let me know.

In 1980, three little birds told Bob Marley every little thing was gonna be all right. A year later, he was dead. Birds are idiots.

Thinking about it, the *worst* trick I ever pulled was convincing people I don't exist.

Man blames most accidents on fate but feels a more personal responsibility when he makes a hole-in-one on the golf course.

I'm worried my life is a *Choose Your Own Adventure* story, in which I make a series of bad decisions and eventually get eaten by dinosaurs.

One potato, two potato, three potato, four. Who am I kidding? Just one potato – I live alone.

'Will you miss me?' is a good way to bid farewell to a firing squad.

Men have feelings too. For example, we feel hungry.

Pick-up lines for old people: Hey baby, you better call life alert, because I've fallen for you and can't get up.

Why did the golfer wear two pairs of trousers? Because he might get a hole in one.

'Very little scares me,' said my new girlfriend. 'Great,' I thought to myself. 'She's going to be terrified when she sees my cock.'

'I just need my own space.' – Selfish astronaut.

What is only a small box but can weigh over a hundred pounds? A scale.

If you play country and western albums backwards, you end up happy, but with a strange feeling that things are about to go wrong.

Newsnight + *University Challenge* x CBeebies = *Question Time*

A lamb follows Mary to school and they write a nursery rhyme. But when I do it…

Thanks for sending a second text correcting your typo. I would've never broken the elaborate code of a single misspelled word without it.

What happens when the smog lifts over Los Angeles? UCLA.

When I die, I give my friends permission to change my Facebook status to 'is chillin' with Jesus'.

Idea for a TV show: Lip-readers follow commuters for a day and contestants guess how many times they say 'you're an idiot' under their breath.

I was an accountant from the age of twenty to the age of thirty, before I was sacked for no apparent reason. What a waste of fourteen years that was.

Whenever I have a one-night stand, I always use protection. A fake name and a fake number.

I just started following the French military on Twitter. They're famous for retweeting.

When it comes to a battle with words I'm always ready to mumble.

I see these mums who can do everything and I think … I should have them do some stuff for me.

The least helpful advice I've ever received was 'never be complaisant'.

Nine months before I was born, I went to this awesome party with my dad, and I left with my mum.

I saw two Siamese twins fighting last night. They ended up bleeding to death after I'd separated them.

Imagine owning a parrot and *not* teaching it to say 'I'm not a parrot, I'm your father. Your drinks were spiked and the doctor's on his way.'

This is how my week goes: Mooooonnnnnddaaaaaayyyyyy Tueeeesssdaaaaaaayyyyyy Weeedddnnnesssdaaaaaayyyyyy Thursssssdaaaaaayyyyyy FridaySaturdaySunday.

I can't understand sign language, but somehow I knew the deaf guy at work thought I was a wanker.

What's the difference between you and eggs? Eggs get laid and you don't.

If Al Gore tried his hand at making music, his album would be called Algorithms.

I just wish pictures and mirrors could agree on what I actually look like.

There's no greater insult than being burgled and finding your DVD collection completely untouched.

I just read a Facebook status that said 'Yes! I have just past my English exam.' Fuck knows how.

If you're drunk, simply place a beermat under one of your feet, as you would with a wobbly table.

I don't like morning people… Or mornings… Or people…

I love watching *The Simpsons*. They never get old.

How do locomotives hear? Through their engineers.

I do all my own stunts, but never intentionally.

I was getting ideas above my station, but now I've lost my train of thought.

I'm sure it was my two-year-old son who stole my pen. It's written all over his face.

I buy all my guns from a bloke called T-Rex. He's a small-arms dealer.

Suicide bomber: 'Everyone has one minute to get out of the pet store!' Turtle: 'You bastard…'

If you're on the treadmill next to me, the answer is 'Yes. We are racing.'

Just joined a gym in case I ever get bored of showering alone.

What's a royal pardon? It's what the Queen says after she burps.

Do you want to speak to the manager or someone who knows what's going on?

I say potato, you say 100 per cent organic Jersey Royals, served dauphinoise-style. You've changed.

There's someone for everyone, and the person for you is a psychiatrist.

Did you hear about the Italian chef that died? He pasta way. We cannoli do so much. His legacy will become a pizza history.

I used to do drugs – I still do, but I used to, too.

Fat guy: What are you looking at? Me: The reason double doors were invented.

'Doctor, I can't pronounce my Fs, Ts and Hs.' 'Well, you can't say fairer than that, then.'

What did Jay-Z call his girlfriend before getting married? Feyoncé.

My friend has got an excellent nose for wine. It's shaped like a corkscrew.

Harry and Sam are on the beach, and Harry can't understand why Sam is getting so much female attention. 'It's simple,' says Sam. 'Just stick a potato down your bathing trunks and walk around for a while.' Harry takes this advice, sticks a potato down his trunks and parades up and down the shoreline. However, he fails to arouse any female interest at all. Discouraged, he goes back to Sam, who immediately identifies the problem. 'You're meant to put the potato down the *front* of your trunks...'

There was a couple who were in the iron and steel business. She did the ironing while he went out stealing.

Three words to ruin a man's ego ... 'Is it in?'

Which candles burn longer, beeswax or tallow? Neither, they both burn shorter.

Where do naughty rays of light go? Prism.

Think my gene pool may have been one of those above-ground ones.

Reality TV idea: Producers compete to devise a reality TV show so bad, even Channel 5 turns it down. Winner gets a job with ITV.

One in ten mates is hated by the other nine. I can't wait to find out who it is when the boys come back from their lads' holiday.

Why do men get their great ideas in bed? Because they're plugged into a genius!

When life gives you lemons, just add vodka.

Why can't your nose be twelve inches long? Because then it would be a foot.

'Never Eat Stolen Wheat.' – Moral compass.

You know when you walk into a room and forget why you went in? That's God, playing The Sims, cancelling your action.

'Please don't see me, please don't see me, please don't see me...' 'Heyyyyy!' 'Shit...'

I only drink on two occasions: 1. When it's my birthday, and 2. When it's not.

My local family butcher's has been in business since 1878, so if I ever decide my family needs butchering, I'll probably use them.

'Nobody remembers who came second.' – Lazy statisticians.

The bee holding its breath underwater in my local pool last week is still there today. Must have set a new world record by now.

A clever person solves a problem. A wise person avoids it. A stupid person makes it.

An onion just told me a joke. I don't know whether to laugh or to cry.

I've found a new hobby: when you have to give your digital signature when signing for a parcel, draw the best cock and balls in the box.

The teacher asked, 'Give me an example of a coincidence?' Student replied, 'My mum and dad got married on the same date.'

I look forward to paying off all my debt and finally getting back to just being broke.

Idea for a horror film: Man goes on holiday just as the weather improves at home.

Just having some professional photos taken in case I ever go missing.

I like to think of all crying babies as the child I never had.

Diarrhoea is hereditary; it runs in your jeans.

I told my mum I'd opened a theatre. She said, 'Are you having me on?' I said, 'I'll give you an audition but I'm not promising anything.'

The last time I called 'shotgun', we had rented a limo, so I screwed up.

I play triangle in a reggae band … I stand at the back and ting.

'One man's trash is another man's treasure' is a great saying, but a terrible way to tell your kids that they're adopted.

'Four more years! Four more years!' – Parole board.

Changing my name to Reason. Because no one ever listens to me.

Why did the blonde snort Splenda? She thought it was diet coke.

What happened when Jesus wanted to swim?

Once I painted a girl in the nude. I almost froze to death.

So I went to the dentist. He said, 'Say "aaah".' I said, 'Why?' He said, 'My dog's died.'

My cooking is so awesome, even the smoke alarm cheers me on.

Dear vegetarians, if you're trying to save the animals, why are you eating their food?

Why do Mexicans never cross the border in groups of three? Because the sign says no tres-passing.

Those who say they 'sleep like a baby' haven't got one.

Just got off the phone with my mum. She had a nice talk.

What is the definition of confidence? When your wife catches you in bed with another woman and you slap her on the ass and say, 'You're next, baby!'

People are like snowflakes: nice for a while, but you wouldn't want to see them every day.

An electron is driving down a motorway, and a policeman pulls him over. The policeman says, 'Sir, do you realise you were travelling at 130km per hour?' The electron goes, 'Oh great, now I'm lost.'

Life's too short to get you many points in Scrabble.

I used to be able to make ends meet. But now they just stare at each other awkwardly from across the room.

I probably spend more time than I should worrying about whether Inspector Gadget truly made the most of his abilities.

Pro-gas-ti-na-tion. Waiting to fill up your tank in the hope that the petrol price might actually go down.

Shoving an Action Man head first halfway up your arse provides a useful pair of miniature emergency legs.

Jokes about stuttering – hahahahaha!

A company sports day is a fun way to find out which members of staff didn't get enough love as children.

I got a new car for the wife. What a great trade.

The first rule of Hypochondria Club is probably not worth remembering because this cold's going to kill me before the next meeting.

My income seems to be the only thing I can't live without or within.

You don't have to be crazy to work here. We'll train you.

Laughter at the expense of others is the best medicine.

I hate people who get my hopes up. Like those bastards who install a light in the middle of a tunnel.

Never ask for directions from a starfish.

What's long and hard and has cum in it? A cucumber.

The man who created the thesaurus has died. He'll be fondly remembered, commemorated, memorialised, recalled and recollected.

'How much can you press?' is a good question to ask if you want to look tough at Flower Press Club.

Whenever there's a long pause in a conversation, I just start barking. Because if there's one thing I can't stand, it's awkward silence.

What's the difference between a tyre and 365 condoms? One's a Goodyear and the other is a fucking good year.

Just implementing my 100th contingency plan of the day.

My family's idea of a Happy Meal is no fighting before dessert.

Did you hear about the jurisprudence fetishist? He got off on a technicality.

If you have a funny sneeze, the world laughs with you, not ATCHOOO!

I want to open up a store next to Forever 21 and call it Finally 22.

'Two drifters off to see the world' is my favourite lyric about a pair of chocolate bars on a gap year.

I just found out milkshakes don't come from breakdancing cows and I don't think I'll trust my parents ever again.

I think my wife is a magician. She can produce four different arguments out of one single glance at a pair of tits.

Why are nursery teachers so good? They make the little things count.

I was adopted at birth and have never met my mum. That makes it very difficult to enjoy any striptease.

My will is mostly just things I borrowed from my neighbours.

My New Year's resolution was to lose twenty pounds by the end of summer. I've only got thirty pounds to go.

What's soft and warm when you go to bed, but hard and stiff when you wake up? Vomit.

How do you find a blind man in a nudist colony? It's not hard.

What might a farmer put on his CV? Works well with udders.

Dieting is wishful shrinking.

Why did the boy drop his ice cream? Because he was hit by a bus.

What do you call a little Mexican? A paragraph, because he's not quite an essay.

Did you guys hear about the cannibal that made a bunch of businessmen into chilli? I guess he liked seasoned professionals.

'Where do you see yourself in five lives' time?' – Buddhist interview question.

'I wasn't that drunk...' 'Dude, you congratulated a potato on getting a part in *Toy Story*!'

Fun fact: Only one word in the English language is ever pronounced correctly, and that word is correctly.

I remember when yoga was called Twister.

Honesty is the best policy. Unless you want people to like you.

Girl, did it hurt when you fell from heaven because – wait, you're from heaven? Are you a ghost?! I'm not sure this is a good idea.

For those waiting for me to go out of my mind: it may take longer. The exits are not clearly marked.

A little boy at a wedding looks at his mother and says, 'Mummy, why does the girl wear white?' His mum replies, 'The bride is in white because she's happy and this is the happiest day of her life.' The boy thinks about this, and then says, 'Well then, why is the boy wearing black?'

After finishing ten pints I was weaving dangerously in the middle of the road. I thought, 'It'd probably be safer to make this cane chair at home.'

I work awfully hard trying to disguise the fact that I'm a lazy bastard.

If Jon Bon Jovi married Bonnie Tyler, Bono, Simon Le Bon and Bon Iver, his name would become Jon Bonnie Bono Le Bon Bon Bon Jovi.

You can always spot the living dead by their wedding ring.

When I took my items to the till in a spiritualist shop earlier I saw a sign that said 'Queue from the other side'. So I killed myself.

I used go out with an anaesthetist – she was a local girl.

This gin and tonic is 91 calories. This banana is 105 calories. My doctor told me to make the healthy choice. I love my doctor.

'We need to talk' is a good thing to say if you're about to break up with a mime artist.

Laughing at your own jokes is a good way of saying 'I'll laugh at anything', which some people find incredibly attractive.

I was driving past the shops today when I saw a sign that said, 'Breakfast Here!' So I did and the car behind went into the back of me.

What kind of band can't play music? A rubber band.

'I just want sex, no strings attached.' – Deluded puppet.

I organised a threesome last night. There were a couple of no-shows, but I still had a great time.

All my wife does is rabbit, rabbit, rabbit. It's costing me a fortune in batteries.

If you describe yourself as a Marmite person and you're not actually a person made out of Marmite, I hate you.

Give a man a fish and he'll eat for a day. Teach a man to fish and you can burgle his house at weekends.

Never put off until tomorrow something you can put off until the day after tomorrow.

Weather forecast: Expect a light flurry of guesswork, followed by a sudden downpour of viewers' photos, ending with a brief, sunny smile.

Surgeons only wear masks so they can pretend they're master criminals stealing precious artefacts from the patient's body while they sleep.

Swiss cheese is a rip-off – it's the only cheese I can bite into and miss.

Remember kids, if a stranger offers you free drugs … take them and say thank you, because drugs are expensive.

Alcohol doesn't solve any problems … but then again, neither does milk.

Did you hear about the man who got cooled to absolute zero? He's 0K now.

At what point does a lamb become a sheep? When it's had its Baaaaa-Mitzvah!

I'm pretty sure God created only six days. Monday was definitely made by Satan.

When your chest starts to look like an upside-down version of their logo, it's time to stop eating at McDonald's.

My cinque stagioni pizza is over-seasoned.

How dare you incinerate that I don't know big words?

What did one tampon say to the other? Nothing; they were both stuck-up bitches.

If you drop out of school, just remember two things: 1. You tried your best, and 2. I don't like pickles on my Big Mac.

I really hope Bono finds what he's looking for before he gets so old he forgets what it is.

The more I think about it, the more I think I'd *immediately* tell Mum the babysitter was dead.

I enjoy watching wrestling a lot more if I think of it as competitive hugging.

I work in McDonald's and a customer was rude to me today, so I got him back by not putting any Coke in his drink. Just ice was served.

If Spiderman was real, and I was a criminal, and he shot me with his web, I'd say, 'Dude, thanks for the hammock.'

I find light snow unsettling.

Have you guys heard the story about the butter? You know what, never mind. I don't want to spread it around.

High-wire artists hate it when their cable goes out.

Why did the strawberry call 999? It was in a jam.

Why is Bon Jovi's bed always messy? Because he doesn't think it matters if you make it or not.

My wife is a water sign. I'm an earth. Together we make mud.

What did the ceiling say to the chandelier? You're the only bright spot in my life.

I said to the girl in the shop, 'I want to buy a hat.' She said, 'Fedora?' I said, 'No, for myself.'

It's always awkward ending phone calls with loved ones. I'm always saying 'I love you' and they're like, 'Erm … thank you for choosing Domino's.'

What did one flower say to the other flower? 'Hey, bud.'

What's the difference between a weasel and a stoat? A weasel is weasel-y recognised and a stoat is stoat-ally different.

It's sad but strangely fitting when an actor's one last job before dying is acting in a 'one last job' movie.

The awkward moment when you're that one friend who always gives relationship advice but is still single.

How does Moses make his tea? Hebrews it.

The easiest way to find something lost around the house is to buy a replacement.

Did you hear about the man who survived mustard gas and pepper spray? They say he's a seasoned veteran.

Sorry to hear you're going through a tough time. I once had to explain *The Usual Suspects* to my sister, so I know how you feel.

To all those who received a book from me as a Christmas present ... They are due back at the library today.

Sometimes the first step to forgiveness is understanding that the other person is a complete idiot.

I'm flexible. First I get bent out of shape and then I tie myself up in knots.

I brag that my son handles financial transactions for a multi-billion-pound corporation. It's easier than saying he is a cashier at McDonald's.

Looking at the state of sun-dried tomatoes, it's probably time they played safe and used fake tan instead.

Brownies *are* a health food ... if you count mental health.

For every action, there is a corresponding over-reaction.

The boss just put me in charge of obeying him.

The best way to avoid a cold is washing your hands and never having children.

Revolving doors are great for when you get to work and then decide to go back home the moment you step in the building.

How many teenage girls does it take to screw in a light bulb? Two: one to screw it in, and one to take a picture.

If you're having second thoughts, you're two ahead of most people.

For those of you wondering what it's like to be married: I just found out this morning that I'm on day three of an argument I didn't know I was having.

If at first you don't succeed, sleep with whoever makes the decisions and try again.

Silent letters are just mime artists without the silly clothes.

Why don't orphans play baseball? They don't know where home is.

'So what's your name short for?' I asked the girl at the bar. 'Same as everyone's,' she said. 'Practicality.'

I wanted to have sex with my girlfriend, but she was on her period. So I had to pull some strings.

My girlfriend says the new breast implants make her feel uncomfortable. But I think I look sexy.

'Why are you impersonating a police officer?' asked the cop. 'Because I'm drunk,' I replied. 'What's your excuse?'

A fool is a 37th-floor window washer who steps backs to see his handiwork.

Dads don't want much. They just hope you'll be happy … and you'll never call while the game's on.

What did the peanut say to the walnut? Nothing. Nuts can't talk.

Early to bed and early to rise … proves man has no interest.

I haven't looked back since I stopped wearing retrospectacles.

I've woken up looking like a badly dubbed advert for German cleaning products.

I went for a job as a gold prospector, but it didn't pan out.

When God closes a door, He usually makes sure my fingers are in it.

Why do they call it the Wonderbra? When you take it off, you wonder where your tits went.

Fun fact: If you play every Beatles song backwards, you can hear the sound of your girlfriend closing the front door and never coming back.

If I had to guess, I'm pretty sure the person who came up with the spelling of 'February' also had something to do with 'Wednesday'.

Show your staff they're more than just employees by following them home and sending them love poetry.

Why did the carpenter fall asleep on the job? He was board.

My mate didn't think having six fingers was much of a deformity. Until I pointed out that they were on his foot.

If you've kidnapped hundreds of doves but now regret doing so, funerals offer a great opportunity to release them without raising suspicion.

It takes thirty-seven muscles to frown at someone, but only five to punch them in the face.

The winner in most divorce cases is the house-keeper.

The other day someone left a piece of plasticine in my dressing room. I didn't know what to make of it.

The bit in *Snow White* when the dwarfs think she's dead, put her in a glass coffin and stare at her for days is lovely and not creepy at all.

I went to Blackpool on holiday and knocked at the first boarding house that I came to. A woman stuck her head out of an upstairs window and said, 'What do you want?' 'I'd like to stay here.' 'OK. Stay there.'

What did the penis say to the vagina? 'Don't make me come in there.'

When I see an advert saying, 'You wouldn't eat a table-spoon of salt!' I just assume they've never seen me swim in the sea when I'm drunk.

What do you get when you cross a donkey and an onion? A piece of ass that'll bring a tear to your eye.

Why did the hippie drown? Because he was too far out, man.

If anyone sends me a work email after midnight, I assume they've just murdered someone and plan to use me as an alibi.

I called the waiter and said, 'This chicken I've got is cold.' He said, 'I should think so. It's been dead for two weeks.' 'Not only that,' I said. 'It's got one leg shorter than the other.' He said, 'What do you want to do, eat it or dance with it?'

If you play She Loves Me, She Loves Me Not with actual people, it's a definite She Loves Me Not by the second arm.

1. Go to police station. 2. Say a gang mugged you. 3. Describe your own relatives to police sketch artist. 4. Claim free family portrait.

Why was the orphan so successful? When they told him 'go big or go home', he only had one option.

What do you call an epileptic in a vegetable garden? Seizure salad.

What do you call a nun in a wheelchair? Holy roller.

I was a premature baby. My father wasn't expecting me.

I'm working out right now. I'm exercising my eyebrow muscles by raising them high. Try it; you'll be surprised!

You can lead a horse to water, but a pencil must be led.

If you watch *Titanic* backwards, it's about a boat that rises from the sea and saves people.

I'm looking for a job where I am politely ignored and left to my own devices. With unlimited internet access, doughnuts and coffee.

I heard a rumour that Cadbury is bringing out an oriental chocolate bar. Could be a Chinese Wispa.

When I heard that oxygen and magnesium hooked up, I was like OMg.

A friend in need is a friend worth hiding from.

It's not easy to admit being wrong. That's why I prefer to chase people, pour glitter on their heads and run away.

They say you need to listen to what your body is telling you. But mine just points and laughs.

How is pubic hair like parsley? You push it to the side before you start eating.

A seal walks into a club.

You are invited to my recycling party on Saturday at 8 p.m. Bring a bottle.

Butterflies aren't what they used to be.

An invisible man married an invisible woman. The kids were nothing to look at either.

Why did the homeless man vote for Obama? Because he promised change.

'It's Raining, It's Pouring' is probably my favourite nursery rhyme about an old man dying alone during a storm.

Just called the depression helpline. Sadly, even the phone lines are down.

'Damn, I forgot to update my Facebook status saying I was at the gym … Now this whole workout was a waste!' – Douche.

It's Shark Week so I'm taking some lawyers to lunch.

Batman came up to me and he hit me over the head with a vase and he went, 'T'PAU!' I said, 'Don't you mean KA-POW?' He said, 'No, I've got china in my hand.'

Did you hear about the man who enjoyed having sex with fruit? Some people say he's not too weird, but I still think he's fucking bananas.

I love Hallowe'en … the cobwebs in my house just become decorations.

Which sexual position creates the ugliest kids? Ask your parents.

'Mwahahahahaha!' – Evil laugh of someone who finds air-kissing funny.

What did the baby corn ask the mother corn? Where is Pop Corn?

I've been around the block a few times. I forgot where I live.

Too much business. Not enough monkey.

So the bad news is I got a little tipsy last night. It worked out though. When I walked across the dance floor I won the dancing contest.

I'm not saying it's hot in my house today, but two hobbits just walked past and threw a ring in through the window.

Here's a quick laugh. Do this tomorrow. Walk into an antiques shop and shout, 'What's new?'

'It's the thought that counts' is such a nice way of saying 'You've let me down again, you massive idiot.'

I hate when I ask a friend what his secret is and he says he killed his aunt for the inheritance but I just meant how does he stay so trim.

Just so you know, when people ask where you were on 9/11, they're actually FBI agents trying to see if you were involved.

'Quit while you're ahead,' my dad used to always say to me. It's no wonder I never won any races.

The last time anyone told me I looked hot, I was in a sauna.

David Cameron, Nick Clegg and Ed Miliband were on a frozen lake not speaking to each other. So I thought I'd go over and break the ice.

Avoid awkward silences in interviews by weeping uncontrollably and begging for the job.

Sex is like software: For every person who pays for it there are hundreds getting it for free.

You're like a brother to me. My brother's an idiot.

'Why does everything have to be about you?' – Terrible biographer.

New government regulations say that Santa's helpers must wear a seatbelt when they're on the sleigh. It's elfin safety gone mad.

Sometimes when you are arguing with a fool, he's doing the same thing.

It's so sad that someone gave Bono a *Where's Wally?* book in 1987 and he *still* hasn't found what he's looking for.

Women love a man in uniform. Except for figure skating.

'My bed is half full.' – Lonely optimist.

'I don't know why you bought that laptop, you never use it,' said my wife. She only says that because she checks my browsing history every day.

Twitter's like most parts of London: perfectly nice during the day, absolutely terrifying at night.

'Bad things always happen in trees.' – Depressed squirrel.

'One hundred per cent of accidents occur within the home.' – Hermits.

I like birthdays, but I think too many can kill you.

What is the difference between a tick and a lawyer? A tick falls off you when you die.

What do you call a cow with a twitch? Beef jerky.

I'm not saying my wife's driving is bad … but to cash in on it, I've opened up a florist.

A painter billed me £0 after finishing painting my house. I asked, 'Why £0?' He said, 'Don't worry about the paint, it's on the house.'

When I die, I'm going to have 'free WiFi' written on my tombstone. That way, more people will visit.

The more books about self-made millionaires I read, the more moving to London with just £5 in my pocket seems like a really good idea.

I just saw nine grim reapers walking down the street drinking beer. So either it's a Hallowe'en party or somebody's cat is actually dead.

This little old lady was frightened. She looked at me, she said, 'Do something religious.' So I took up a collection.

If elephants never forget, why do they never write autobiographies? What are they hiding?

You can't buy happiness, but you can buy vodka and that's pretty much the same thing.

I went to buy some camouflage trousers the other day but I couldn't find any.

I wish some of my co-workers weren't allowed in the break room … Because that's who I usually need a break from.

I tripped over someone's bra earlier. I think it was a booby trap.

This guy told me he is the fastest cross-dresser in the world. I said, 'Really?' She said, 'Yes.'

Waitress: Do you have any questions about the menu?
Me: What kind of font is this?

I think all car alarms should be replaced with a recording of a boy's voice crying 'Wolf! Wolf! Wolf!' over and over.

Why couldn't the pirates play cards? They were sitting on the deck.

I've woken up looking like a YouTube comments section.

Why is b always cool? Because it's between ac.

I'm running out of unproductive things to do at work.

Why did the drum take a nap? It was beat.

How does a lead guitar player change a light bulb? He doesn't, he just steals someone else's light.

Don't lead, I'll wander off and get bored. Don't follow, I'll get us both lost. Walk beside me and help me cause trouble.

I can stereotype twice as fast as I can type.

In the fight to stay warm, the gloves are off! Which isn't helping.

What part of the car is the laziest? The wheels, because they are always tired.

I'm not a complete idiot. Some parts are missing.

Teacher: Why's your cat at school today? Tim: My dad said to my mum, 'I'm going to eat that pussy when the kids leave,' so I'm saving him.

My friends think I'm too indecisive. I don't know what to think of that.

I'm starting to worry that the African elephant I adopted five years ago will never think of me as his real father.

When the kitchen smells warm and cosy, it can only mean one thing. We're not in my kitchen.

I can still remember a time when I knew more than my phone.

Petrol prices aren't really that bad when you remember that you're essentially buying badass dinosaurs in liquid form.

Complaining to the police about something you've read on the internet is like suing a premium-rate sex line for sexual harassment.

Why are there only 239 beans in Irish stew? Because one more, and it'd be too farty.

I want my tombstone to say 'Don't just stand there, water my flowers.'

'May I take your coat, sir?' – Good waiter/Polite mugger.

What do you call water that bounces? Spring water.

What did the number 0 say to number 8? 'Nice belt!'

Why didn't Mr Clean's wife ever get pregnant? He comes in a bottle.

If you stain your clothes while eating, don't panic. Get two bottles of white wine. Drink them quickly and you won't give a fuck.

Everyone has a photographic memory, some just don't have film.

Why did the TV cross the road? Because it wanted to be a flat screen.

You had me at 'hello'. You lost me at 'Have you been mis-sold PPI?'

Two cannibals are eating a clown. One says to the other, 'Does this taste funny to you?'

I went to the doctor's. He said, 'I'd like you to lie on the couch.' I said, 'What for?' He said, 'I'd like to sweep the floor.'

You can take the boy out of the country, but you can't if it's a porcelain boy stuffed with cocaine.

I went to a pet shop. I said, 'Can I buy a goldfish?' The guy said, 'Do you want an aquarium?' I said, 'I don't care what star sign it is.'

I had a meal last night. I ordered everything in French, surprising everybody. It was a Chinese restaurant.

If you're seeing things running through your head, who ya gonna call? Probably a psychiatrist.

My neighbour's car just slept through its alarm, but luckily two guys shook it awake and took it wherever it needed to go.

I can never tell if a mother duck is being dutifully followed by her ducklings or chased by a gang of young duck criminals.

A co-worker announced he's getting married. I told him how happy my marriage has made me. But he's still going through with it anyway.

Diamonds aren't a girl's best friend ... I've never heard my wife talking about them behind their backs.

My friend drowned in a bowl of muesli. A strong currant pulled him in.

These shot glasses are terrible. Full of bullet holes.

Dear Microsoft Word, I'm pretty sure I spelled my name correctly.

Imagine being a chef and not playing pass-the-parcel with an onion at least once a week.

What do you give a cannibal who is late for dinner? The cold shoulder.

What do you call a cheap circumcision? A rip-off.

Worth remembering that spiders can see in the dark, so if we do eat them in our sleep, it's their own stupid fault.

Why did the class clown take a computer to school? Her mum told her to bring in an apple for the teacher.

Home alone, having a heart attack – HAHAHA!

Regular naps prevent old age ... especially if you take them while driving.

I always sit in the back of a plane. It's much safer. You never hear of a plane backing into a mountain.

The Hollywood actress liked her tenth husband so much she decided to keep him for an extra fortnight.

If employers say they're looking for the X factor, turn up dressed as Leona Lewis and they'll laugh and laugh and beg you to start tomorrow.

Yesterday I fired my cleaner. I'm really glad that's done and dusted.

Recreate the magic of Christmas by slumping on the sofa and moaning about whatever's on TV.

What did the debater say after getting stabbed during an argument? Good point.

Men get frustrated because they don't understand how women think. Women get frustrated because they understand how men think.

For most people, Burns Night comes just before Australia Day. For English backpackers, it's often the other way round.

Sadly, my only steady girlfriend was also the most unstable.

So I got home, and the phone was ringing. I picked it up, and said, 'Who's speaking please?' And a voice said, 'You are.'

A bargain is something you don't need at a price you can't resist.

Dead budgie for sale. Not going cheap.

It's so rude when people arriving at court for sentencing are 'greeted by hordes of photographers' and don't even say hello back.

Trust me, you'd never eat mobsters again if you saw them being made.

To get your porn star name, take the number of times you've had sex in the past week and you're not a porn star, are you? Get back to work.

When a magician says his bedroom is 'where the magic happens' he means actual magic tricks, because have you ever met a magician?

Every warning label has an awesome backstory.

It's a ten-minute walk from my house to the pub. Weirdly, it's a two-hour walk from the pub to my house.

What did Earth say to the other planets? Wow, you guys have no life.

It's so obvious that cryptic crosswords had absolutely zero friends at crossword school.

Two koalas, sitting in a tree, K-I-P-P-I-N-G.

You wouldn't like me when I'm angry. Mind you, I'm even more annoying when I'm happy, so just go for it and make me angry.

I bought some Armageddon cheese today, and it said on the packet 'best before end'.

Why did the boy fall off the swing? He didn't have any arms.

If a friend says 'pictures or it didn't happen', murder him and don't take any pictures.

What's long and hard and full of seamen? A submarine.

Police officer: Freeze! Criminal: Everybody clap your hands!

Doctors: Put patients at ease by doing jazz hands immediately after putting on surgical gloves.

'Age is just a number…' 'Yeah, and weed is just a plant.'

I'm no expert, but I'm starting to think North and South Korea might never remarry.

When I was a boy, I lay in my twin-sized bed and wondered where my brother was.

How does a train sneeze? 'Ah-choo-choo!'

Whenever someone rings the doorbell, my dog always assumes it's for him.

Spoiler alert: Don't leave milk out of the fridge for too long in warm weather.

This dinosaur handing out flyers and shouting about 'Monster Savings' is so clearly not a real dinosaur. Dinosaurs can't talk, for starters.

Dammit, this spermicide didn't work at all. My kids are still here and now they won't stop whining about their eyes burning.

What is the difference between ooooooh and aaaaaaah? About three inches.

You speak in haiku / That is *very* attractive / Said no girl ever

I find mind-readers really annoying, and I bet they don't even know why.

Never get married in college; it's hard to get a start if a prospective employer finds out you've already made one mistake.

People who exist in a parallel universe are never allowed to touch each other.

I wonder if I'll ever stare out of a plane window and not pretend I've just made a terrible decision in a Hollywood rom-com.

'You can't just expect everything on a plate.' – Good Parent/Bad Waiter.

Gently whispering 'I only do this to be close to people' is a nice way to ease the tension on a packed commuter train.

Pretzels are the show-off contortionists of the baking world and deserve to be eaten.

Which runs faster, hot or cold water? Hot, because you can catch cold.

I hate to brag, but I still have the credit rating of a much younger man.

Just for the record, the weather today is calm and sunny, but the air is full of bullshit.

'I love what you've done with your hair' will always be my favourite way of saying 'Jesus Christ, what have you done to your hair?!'

'There's a spider in the room!' screamed my wife. 'Get it out, John! Please get it out!' 'I don't know why they turn you on so much,' I said, unzipping my jeans.

You'd never see me run away from a fight. Mostly because I'd faint immediately.

A friend of mine always wanted to be run over by a steam train. When it happened, he was chuffed to bits.

Freak out your neighbours. Name your WiFi 'FBI Surveillance Van'.

I went to a seafood disco last week. I pulled a mussel.

Thumb Wars are sadly inevitable with so many opposable thumbs in the world.

When I asked her to whisper those three little words that would make me walk on air, she said, 'Sure. Go hang yourself.'

A mime will never give you bad advice.

Why do giraffes have long necks? Because they have smelly feet.

It would be more fun to watch out-of-shape people compete in the Olympics.

So, apparently not everyone includes any fights they won at school in the Notable Achievements section of their CV.

From now on I'm only going to buy that fancy water with healthy additives. Like this one here. It's got hops, yeast and malted barley in it.

Wife: I'll be back, honey! Husband: Don't threaten me like that.

Why are there five syllables in the word 'monosyllabic'?

I hate Mondays, Tuesdays, Wednesdays, Thursdays and half of Friday.

I've just seen an advert in my local newspaper: 'Accountant Needed. £35,000–£40,000.' So I phoned them up and said, 'The answer is –£5,000.'

Wife: Baby, I'm pregnant. What do you want it to be? Husband: A joke.

What's orange and sounds like a parrot? A carrot.

There's a green and purple grape. The green grape says to the purple grape, 'Breathe, breathe!'

Some people have a way with words, and other people … oh, uh, no way.

Fun fact: MC Hammer wrote 'U Can't Touch This' when he worked in a museum.

Why should honeymoons only last six days? Because seven days makes a hole weak.

Critical Mass (noun): Twitter.

Inarticulate? I don't even know the meaning of the word.

I went into a shop and I said, 'Can someone sell me a kettle?' The bloke said, 'Kenwood?' I said, 'OK, where is he then?'

My dad was telling me about the good old days. 'We used to watch porn without the annoying pop-ups.'

There's no sadder sight than a hippo so hungry he'll eat marbles for the entertainment of children.

What goes up and down but never moves? Stairs.

'101 is the loneliest number.' – Neglected Dalmatian.

Men say women should come with instructions … but what's the point of that? Have you ever seen a man actually read the instructions?

What happens in Vegas stays in your credit rating for up to six years.

The real tragedy of *Goldilocks and the Three Bears* is that Mr and Mrs Bear, a young married couple, already sleep in separate beds.

I've woken up looking like the indie band who refused to sell their one big hit to a TV advert and now work in a supermarket.

Teach pickpockets a lesson by keeping your bag and pockets full of mousetraps at all times.

I often wonder what happens if you get scared half to death twice?

There are lots of up-and-coming actors in the porn industry.

I've often wanted to drown my troubles, but I can't get my wife to go swimming.

Why was the leper hockey game cancelled? There was a face-off in the corner.

'Leave it. She's not worth it.' L'Oreal model advises a friend not to fight.

It breaks my heart that pirates spend their whole lives following a map, when the real treasure is the friendships they build along the way.

If a tree falls in a forest and no one is around to hear it, does it write a blog describing its crippling loneliness?

Climate is what you expect: weather is what you get.

Michelangelo's finest work is something everyone can look up to.

What goes ha, ha plonk? Someone laughing their head off.

Make commuting fun by playing musical chairs between stops.

Just so you know, *West Side Story* gives a very misleading idea of how much singing and dancing went on among 1950s New York street gangs.

What's an acceptable amount of nail varnish to wear to football these days?

What do you call a virgin on a waterbed? A cherry float.

Hyperbole is easily the best word ever.

I've woken up looking like a murder they tried to disguise as an accident.

People who sleep in socks must be very, very small.

Why don't they have gambling in Africa? There are too many cheetahs.

My boss: I've noticed you nodding off during meetings recently. Are you getting enough sleep? Me: Not really, the meetings are a lot shorter these days.

I just found out my girlfriend has 50,000 bees. I think she's a keeper.

'Do you like water coolers?' – My disastrous attempt to start a water-cooler conversation.

Wine only contains 1 per cent of the recommended daily intake of calcium, so remember to drink 100 glasses every day.

My new thesaurus is terrible. It's also terrible.

Childbirth is an out-of-body experience.

Fun fact: The eighth deadly sin is forgetfulness.

What room can't you enter? A mushroom.

What happens when Batman sees Catwoman? The Dark Knight Rises.

How do you make a tissue dance? Put a little boogie in it.

Why do dragons sleep during the day? So they can fight knights.

The reason grandchildren and grandparents get along so well is because they have a common enemy.

What starts with E, ends with E and only has one letter? An envelope.

A man walked into a therapist's office looking very depressed. 'You've got to help me. I can't go on like this.' 'What's the problem?' the doctor enquired. 'Well, I'm thirty-five years old and I still have no luck with the ladies. No matter how hard I try, I just seem to scare them away.' 'My friend, this is not a serious problem. You just need to work on your self-esteem. Each morning, I want you to get up and run to the bathroom mirror. Tell yourself that you are a good person, a fun person, and an attractive person. But say it with real conviction. Within a week you'll have women buzzing all around you.' The man seemed content with this advice and walked out of the office a bit excited. Three weeks later he returned with the same downtrodden expression on his face. 'Did my advice not work?' asked the doctor. 'It worked all right. For the past several weeks I've enjoyed some of the best moments in my life with the most fabulous looking women.' 'So, what's your problem?' 'My wife is getting fed up.'

'I'm not saying a damned word until my lawyer gets here!' is a cool but ultimately doomed way to start a job interview.

It's so sad how history has completely forgotten Catherine the Great's little brother, George the Mediocre.

I wish whoever convinced superheroes that capes were a good idea had been involved in more big decisions.

What is Moby Dick's dad's name? Papa Boner.

During exams, students look up for inspiration, down in desperation, and left and right for information.

As I watched the dog chasing his tail, I thought, 'Dogs are so easily amused.' Then I realised I was watching the dog chase his tail.

What's brown and sounds like a bell? Dung.

I haven't slept for ten days, because that would be too long.

If a man said he'll fix it, he will. There is no need to remind him every six months about it.

Why was the woman fired from the car assembly line? She was caught taking a brake.

Fun fact: Breaking a mirrorball causes 7,000,000,000 years' bad luck.

What has holes all over and holds water? A sponge.

What do you see when you drop a piano down a mine-shaft? A flat minor.

I told my boss I was handing in my gun and badge today. 'Jesus Christ,' he said. 'You're only a security guard, why the hell have you got a gun?'

When the police arrived to arrest the quack doctor at his clinic, they couldn't find him. He had already ducked out.

Just found out that in the 1970s not everybody was kung-fu fighting and now I'm wondering how many other lies Carl Douglas told.

Called my boss and asked, 'What's the difference between work and your daughter? I will not be coming into work today.'

Somebody actually complimented me on my driving today. They left a little note on the windscreen. It said 'Parking Fine.'

I've thought long and hard, and have decided on my New Year's resolution: 1024 x 768.

The saddest part of living in a one-horse town is knowing it will soon be a no-horse town because the horse has nobody to procreate with.

I cannot believe a woman has started breastfeeding in this restaurant ... Now I have to move to a different table so I can get a better view.

Police: What's your emergency? Me: Two girls are fighting over me! Police: So what's the problem, sir? Me: The ugly one is winning!

A recent survey shows that sperm banks beat blood banks in contributions ... hands down.

I'll never need a shrink as long as my friends tell me what's wrong with me for free.

'Are you a man or a mouse?!' the method actor asked himself as he prepared for his new job at Disney World.

If age is just an attitude, I could use an attitude adjustment.

I like to play blackjack. I'm not addicted to gambling, I'm addicted to sitting in a semi-circle.

If life gives you melons, you might be dyslexic.

Misfortune is the kind of fortune that never misses.

I hold the world record for Most Fictitious World Records.

I had to tell my patient I'd dreadfully messed up his plastic surgery. I'll never forget the look on his elbow.

If a pair of socks is thrown away because one of them has a hole, the other gets bitter and resentful and they never speak again.

Some lettuce, an egg, and a tap had a race. What was the result? The lettuce came in ahead, the egg got beaten and the tap's still running.

So I went to the doctor and he said, 'You've got hypochondria.' I said, 'Oh no, not that as well.'

'Brrr, it's a bit cold. How do we work again?' – Trains.

We had a power outage last week and my PC, TV and games shut down, so I had to talk to my family for a few hours. They seem like nice people.

My brother was so mean when I was a child. He used to glue the pages of his porn magazines together so I couldn't look at them.

'I didn't spend seven years in medical school for you to come in here telling Mr Mister jokes.' – Doctor.

I asked a builder if he could install windows for me and he quoted me £4,000! PC World did it for £150. Goes to show, if you shop around you can save a few quid.

Life is a gift; you never get the one you really wanted.

I think the way I'm eating this banana is making everyone uncomfortable. I should probably at least take a bite.

I've got 999 problems and making hoax calls to the emergency services is all of them.

When I'm lying on my deathbed, my one big regret will be that I'm lying on my deathbed.

Fun fact: The flags placed by various explorers have officially made Antarctica the world's biggest golf course.

What's the difference between a woman in church and a woman in the bath? One has hope in her soul.

I had an embarrassing moment yesterday when I called my boss 'Dad'. She was well pissed off.

North Korea has claimed they are only using their missiles for experimental reasons. They want to see what happens if they nuke the USA.

What's worse than finding a worm in your apple? Lots of things. Watch the news, you idiot.

When is a door not a door? When it's ajar.

Tequila is the Banksy of leaving unexplained marks on my body.

When do you kick a midget in the balls? When he's standing next to your girlfriend saying her hair smells nice.

I thought my wife was having an affair with another man after I found a text on her phone. Fortunately, she's not. It's still the same guy.

What's green and has wheels? Grass, I lied about the wheels.

After a terrible accident during rehearsals for my new play about magicians, the final act is now in two parts.

I used to have a riding school, but business kept falling off.

I wonder how many people really called Steve Miller 'The Space Cowboy' or 'The Gangster of Love' or 'Maurice'. My guess would be zero.

I can count on the finger of one hand the number of times I've used a chainsaw when drunk.

FBI: Make fugitives come to you by replacing your Ten Most Wanted list with a 'Sexy Criminal Mastermind WLTM Similar' online dating ad.

While you're sleeping, xylophones march up and down their page of the dictionary reminding all the other x-words who the real star is.

Birds can be so clever, but the number of emergency landings they make in my garden suggests their air traffic control system's a shambles.

Life is like a box of chocolates. The further through you get, the fewer options are open to you.

Scooby-Doo is a lot more fun once you realise that every episode is just one of Shaggy's stoned hallucinations.

So I started playing the piano and this elephant burst into tears. I said, 'Do you recognise the tune?' He said, 'I recognise the ivory.'

My friend looks just like Brian Blessed, although I wish people would stop telling her.

I'm glad I don't have to hunt for my food. I don't even know where sandwiches live.

Contrary to what most people would say, the most dangerous animal in the world is not the lion or the tiger or even the elephant. It's a shark riding on an elephant's back, just trampling and eating everything they see.

What happens in Vegas, stays in Vegas. Which is a nightmare if you win millions at the casino.

A boiled egg is hard to beat.

I find a duck's opinion of me is very much influenced by whether or not I have bread.

A bunch of my friends are coming over tonight to play on their phones.

Childhood is like being drunk: everyone remembers what you did, except you.

Why are the floors of basketball courts always so damp? The players dribble a lot.

'Be yourself' is about the worst advice you can give to some people.

I do not agree with what you have to say, but I'll defend to the death your right to apologise and accept that I'm never, ever wrong.

The early bird catches the worm. The other birds sleep in, eat a nice brunch and laugh at the insomniac, worm-eating fool.

I suggested to my Thai bride that we have a baby. For some reason she's dead set on adoption.

I appeared in lots of best-dressed lists in my salad days.

What did the judge order in his whisky? Just ice.

People who beat eggs are the worst cowards on Earth.

What is the difference between a genealogist and a gynaecologist? A genealogist looks up your family tree. A gynaecologist looks up your family bush.

When do you go on red and stop on green? When you're eating a watermelon.

I've just won £10 million on the lottery and decided to buy my local Chinese takeaway called 'Happiness'. Your move, philosophers.

Convince people you're a fruit machine by standing in the corner of a pub in a Hawaiian shirt.

Man goes to the doctors, with a strawberry growing out of his head. The doctor says, 'I'll give you some cream to put on it.'

What's 182 feet tall and made out of pepperoni and cheese? The leaning tower of pizza.

Why did the man run around his bed? To catch up on his sleep.

What school do you have to drop out of to graduate from? Parachute school.

My new book, *The Art of Ghost-Writing*, is a flop. I should have got someone else to write it for me.

A severed foot is the ultimate stocking stuffer.

Did I ever tell you my Alzheimer's joke? I can't remember.

Lots of people are terrible at counting calories. And they have the figures to prove it.

I feel sorry for people who don't drink or do drugs. Because someday they're going to be in a hospital bed, dying, and they won't know why.

I order the club sandwich all the time and I'm not even a member. I don't know how I get away with it.

Make crying fun by pretending your tears are two friends racing each other down a water slide.

Dating a single mother: it's like continuing from somebody else's saved game.

There are 400 billion birds in the world, 250,000 planes, and one Superman. So, in answer to your question – probably a bird.

Current relationship status: Just bought my cat an eternity ring.

'I love a girl with a dirty mouth.' – Eager dentist.

I'm at the front of the queue for Paranoids Anonymous. Everyone else is after me.

Why did the girl fall off the swing? Because she had no arms.

Knock, knock. Who's there? Not the girl with no arms.

What do a mole and an eagle have in common? They both live underground, apart from the eagle.

When caterpillars become butterflies, they must wake up, look in the mirror and think, 'Jesus, how much did I drink last night?'

My son asked me what the difference between a pavement and a sidewalk was. 'A firm grasp of the English language,' I replied.

Current relationship status: Just bought a book called *How to Solve Crosswords*.

Alcohol is never the answer … But it does help you forget the question.

Success is like a fart. It only bothers people when it's not their own.

I've completely lost the will to live. Sorry, did I say 'live'? I meant 'work'.

Fun fact: The birth of your first child marks the official start of training for the parents' race at school sports day.

'Children should be seen and not heard.' – Mime parents.

Have you guys heard about the new restaurant on the moon? Early critics say the food is good, but there's no atmosphere.

Bank robbers: Inhaling 500kg of helium just before you enter the bank will both disguise your voice *and* facilitate an airborne getaway.

Driving a convertible at 100mph is such a cool way of hiding the fact you have terrible hair.

Whenever I have to restart my BlackBerry, I text everyone in my phone book. Just to let them know I won't be available for the next hour or so.

The pen is mightier than the sword, according to the proverb. But only if you can write one hell of a convincing letter to an angry samurai.

Gloves are always handy.

I wish there was a thirty-second 'undo' on text messaging.

I lost my wife at the bar. Which is only appropriate, since I found her there.

My wife says she's leaving me because of my addiction to antidepressants. Won't be needing them anymore, then.

I had a vasectomy the other day. Now whenever I come, a little sign saying 'Bang!' pops out.

I phoned the local ramblers club today and this bloke just went on and on.

Video killed the radio star. Years later, DVDs carried out a brutal revenge killing.

I was taking the motorway out of London. A policeman pulled me over and said, 'Put it back.'

Good news: There are hot singles in your area. Bad news: This just increases the likelihood of you being alone forever.

What is Tom Hanks' wireless password? 1forrest1

Hot-air balloon theft. It's on the rise.

Whoever said money can't buy happiness didn't know where to shop.

What is always hot in the refrigerator? Chilli.

Why do scuba divers fall backwards out of boats? If they fell forwards they would still be in the boat.

I just put something that isn't a glove into the glove compartment and I've never felt so alive.

A problem shared is a problem halved. Or doubled if the problem is a contagious disease.

Hear no evil, speak no evil and you'll never be invited to my wife's parties.

If a stork brings white babies, and a blackbird brings black babies, what bird brings no babies? A swallow.

Cryogenics is nothing new. My landlord has been freezing bodies every winter for years.

What has a pee at the end of a tram? A tramp.

Why are hipsters such great assassins? Because they hide the bodies in places no one has ever heard of.

My neighbour was banging on my door at 4 a.m. Good job I was up playing my bagpipes.

If I look tired at the end of the day, it's because I just spent eight solid hours looking busy.

I don't know if any of you saw today's *Jeremy Kyle Show*, but if you did ... Get a life you sad bloody loser.

Pretend you're a bus driver by waving as you pass any vehicle similar to your own.

King-size beds just remind me how cool it would be if we still had giant, rectangular kings.

I think Bigfoot is blurry, that's the problem – it's not the photographer's fault.

Groundhog Day, Super Bowl, Pancake Day, Lent, Valentine's Day. February tries way too hard to be funny to make up for being short.

I once saw a forklift lift a crate of forks. It was way too literal for me.

You can tell a lot about a person by stealing their identity and pretending to be them for the rest of your life.

God is chatting to the Archangel Gabriel. 'Y'know, I just created a 24-hour period of alternating light and darkness.' 'Wow,' replies Gabriel. 'What are you going to do now?' 'I think I'll call it a day,' replies God.

A ventriloquist is telling blonde jokes in a bar when one of his audience, a young blonde lady, stands up and complains. 'I've heard just about enough of your lousy blonde jokes!' she shouts. 'What makes you think you can stereotype women this way? What does a person's hair colour have to do with their worth as a human being?' The ventriloquist is very embarrassed and starts to apologise. The blonde interrupts. 'Stay out of it, mister. I'm talking to the little bastard on your knee.'

What do you call a fake noodle? An impasta.

What did the woman say to the vampire when she woke up with her period? 'I made you breakfast in bed!'

Money can't buy happiness, but it can pay for a professional hitman to kill people who constantly remind you that money can't buy happiness.

He's so tight-fisted he's got varicose veins in his knuckles.

Traces of zebras found in Tesco barcodes.

The worst place to get pins and needles is in the queue for the security scan in an airport.

If you only put your hand to your mouth *after* I see you yawning, it's too late. I've already counted your fillings and decided I hate you.

Sunrises are just as beautiful as sunsets only less crowded.

There was a man who entered a local paper's pun contest. He sent in ten different puns hoping at least one of the puns would win but, unfortunately, no pun in ten did.

I sure will be glad when scientists discover a cure for natural causes.

Just a shot in the dark, but you like drinking tequila with the curtains drawn, don't you?

I went to the dentist the other day. While I was waiting I read some magazines. Isn't it terrible about that *Titanic*?

My fruit and vegetable business has gone into liquidation. We now sell smoothies.

'What you don't know can't hurt you!' is a fun thing to write in the Get Well Soon card of someone who didn't know his brakes needed fixing.

A penny saved is a government oversight.

Who's richer, the butcher, the baker, or the candlestick maker? The baker, because he has lots of dough.

'I'll have what she's having.' – Me, watching a woman having a nervous breakdown.

If I take your advice and grab the bull by the horns, the least you can do is drive me to hospital.

The moon is full of mysterious landscapes and craters. On the bright side, you can see them.

The surgeon asked 'Do you have a dog?' I said, 'Yes, why?' He said, 'If I can't save your leg, do you want me to keep the bone for him?'

Now you know those trick candles that you blow out and a couple of seconds later they come alight again? Well, the other day there was a fire at the factory that makes them.

Time capsules are meant to be fun, but the one in this cemetery's just full of bones. Rubbish.

What's worse than a baby screaming? Two babies screaming.

A woman tells her husband, 'John, that young couple next door seem so in love. Every morning, when he leaves the house, he kisses her goodbye, and every evening, when he comes home, he brings her a dozen roses. Why can't you do that?' 'Well, to be fair,' says John, 'I hardly know the girl.'

At an international medical conference two African surgeons are having an argument. 'I tell you it sounds like "wooooom",' says one. 'You're wrong,' says the other. 'It sounds like "woombba".' 'You're both wrong,' says a passing French surgeon. 'In English it is pronounced "womb".' 'Ridiculous,' replies one of the Africans. 'I'll wager that you've never even seen a wild hippopotamus, let alone heard one fart underwater.'

My daughter walks very quietly whenever she's near the bathroom cabinet. She says she doesn't want to wake the sleeping pills.

Greek people must feel like tampons. They live in one of the most beautiful places in the world, but at the worst period.

My friend just said a film appeals to the child in him. As you can imagine, I'm quite upset that my friend once ate a child.

Brazil's new stadium looks good. I expected the pitch to just be a strip of turf on the edge of the box.

Saying 'beer can' with a British accent sounds like 'bacon' with a Jamaican accent.

'I love this girl, but she doesn't even know I exist.' – Brilliant stalker.

What kind of band doesn't play music? A highbred.

'Wink wink, say no more.' – Someone having a power nap.

Current relationship status: Not bothering to delete internet history.

If anyone performed an autopsy on me right now, they'd think they'd stumbled upon a *Man v. Food* audition gone horribly wrong.

Daylight Savings: I'm all for gaining an hour on the weekend, but why can't we lose the hour at 2 p.m. on a Monday?

My belt holds my trousers up, but the belt loops hold my belt up – so which one's the real hero?

Nudists have successful marriages because neither partner wears the trousers.

Hippopotomonstrosesquippedaliophobia: Fear of long words. Now I know how that word came to mean that.

A guy walks into the psychiatrist wearing only clingfilm for shorts. The shrink says, 'Well, I can clearly see you're nuts.'

Just bought some posh cheesy puffs from Waitrose. They're called Whatwhatwhatsits.

If you're flammable and have legs, you are never blocking a fire exit.

Apparently, you can only say 'Look at you! You got so big!' to children ... Old girlfriends tend to get offended.

It's tragic how the Fresh Prince's mum threw him out and made him live 2,000 miles away, all because he got in one little fight.

Why did the biscuit go to the doctor? Because he was feeling crumby.

Enjoy the thrill of camping without leaving the house by switching off the heating and drinking coffee from a plastic cup.

Their eyes met across a crowded room. Sadly, it was a courtroom and they were finalising their divorce. Terrible mess.

Every person has a story to tell, which is why I never talk to people.

I really wasn't planning on going for a run today but those cops came out of nowhere.

'Are you single?' 'No, I'm plural.' 'No, I meant are you free this Friday?' 'No, I'm expensive.'

'It was the next-door neighbour, in the hallway, with the guitar Alan wouldn't stop playing.' – My next-door neighbour Alan's obituary.

I'm in a same-sex marriage. The sex is always the same.

The 10110010th circle of Hell is for people who write jokes about binary numbers.

If you ever get sad, think of a T-Rex trying to masturbate.

My girlfriend is well pumped up for sex tonight ... I might have to pump her up some more though, I think she's got a slow puncture.

What has four wheels and flies? A rubbish truck.

The older I get, the more I suspect *The Jetsons* was based on nothing more than idle guesswork.

What did one eye say to the other? 'Between you and me, something smells.'

The party's not over till you smile for the mugshot.

Just been playing Candy Crush. Mr Singh wasn't happy with the mess I left on his shop floor though.

My friend and I are moving into a tree house together. I just hope we never fall out.

I wanted to be a milkman, but I didn't have the bottle.

If you hold a seashell to your ear, you can hear the sound of your nephew telling you to stop pretending the seashell's a phone and grow up.

I wanted to give you something you need but I didn't know how to wrap up a bath tub.

Just heard scientologists aren't even fully qualified scientists and now I don't know what to believe.

Some people should use a glue stick instead of a chapstick.

More often than not, the wolf in a sheep's clothing is just trying to keep warm. People are so cynical.

I'm ready to be a parent because I just told the oil-change guy 'no' fifteen times in thirty seconds.

What's worse than spiders on your piano? Crabs on your organ.

My friends refuse to play chess with me. They say I don't understand the rules, but I think it's because I'm too good. I always roll a double six.

I had a bottle of wine and it was beautiful, but now it's all gone and I feel so sad. Tell someone you love them before it's too late.

There were five people under one umbrella. Why didn't they get wet? It wasn't raining.

The saddest day of my childhood was when the other kids told Santa Claus I wasn't real.

A race is about to start. The coach says, 'One … two … three … GO!' and blows the whistle. Everybody except Fred runs. Coach: Fred! Why aren't you running? Fred: Because my number is four.

I have a condition that renders me unable to go on a diet. I get hungry.

My life's like an episode of *Only Fools and Horses*: always trying to get rich and nothing funny has happened since 1989.

What music do chickens listen to? Bach.

Pressing the snooze button is just the first act in a long day of procrastination.

Cameraman targets, by sport: Elvis (cricket); lion (rugby); sexy Brazilian (football); minor British celebrity (tennis).

'The total cost would be £3,000,' said the funeral director. 'That includes digging the grave.' 'Is that the whole thing?' I asked. He replied, 'Yes, that's the hole thing.'

Why are cowgirls bowlegged? Cowboys like to eat with their hats on.

Alcohol is a perfect solvent: It dissolves marriages, families and careers.

I drink too much. The last time I gave a urine sample it had an olive in it.

Keep your friends close and your enemies closer. Then have terrible sex with your enemy – they'll never bother you again. You're welcome.

It's surely no coincidence that dolphins are a) super-intelligent, and b) never even suspected of unsolved murders.

I stepped on a cornflake. Now I'm a cereal killer.

Running away doesn't help you with your problems, unless you're fat.

Dear shaving adverts, stop shaving hairless legs. If you want impress us, please shave a gorilla.

What do you call a woman who sets fire to her phone bills? Bernadette.

Just used my phone to record my wife snoring. She'd kill me if I ever played this in front of her friends. So ... I guess this is goodbye.

I make sure I give my wife a hug every day, as soon as I wake up. I like a good stretch in the morning.

I just ran into one of the Seven Dwarfs. He wasn't happy.

Why can't Barbie get pregnant? Because Ken comes in a different box.

Always make sure a cactus isn't someone having a terrible allergic reaction to acupuncture.

What's the best parting gift? A comb.

Live every day as if it's your last: being spoon-fed dinner by women dressed as nurses.

My son made a 'World's Greatest Father' cup in school today. I don't know why, the stupid brat doesn't have kids.

If you're not part of the solution, you're part of the team I work in.

I do not agree with what you have to say, but I'll defend to the death your right to say it after I've left for the day.

Why did the Oreo go to the dentist? To get his filling.

I said, 'Doctor, I keep getting these dizzy spells.' He said, 'Vertigo?' I said, 'No, I only live up the road.'

I've got the best wife in England. The other one's in Africa.

My wife said she's leaving me because of my ridiculous lies. 'How can you turn your back on the man carrying your child?' I shouted.

I got an ant farm; them fellas didn't grow shit.

It took me so long to pass my Modern Studies exam, they gave me a degree in History.

If you had a donkey and I had a chicken and if your donkey ate my chicken, what would you have? A black eye.

My mate said, 'Make sure you've got nothing on next Saturday, we're going to my mum's fiftieth birthday.' I felt like a right twat, walking in naked.

How does Good King Wenceslas like his pizza? Deep pan, crisp and even.

Why are Native Americans the most successful strippers? Because when they dance, they make it rain.

Why did the basketball player bring his suitcase to his game? Because he travelled a lot.

Beekeeping is just hoarding with a hint of danger.

This shirt is 'dry-clean only' – which means it's dirty.

I was at a garden centre and I asked for something herby. They gave me a Volkswagen with no driver.

Up in the attic earlier with the wife. Old, cold, full of cobwebs, but she's good to the kids.

How do you get a man to stop biting his nails? Make him wear shoes.

Trying to think of something more unnecessary than a bank robber telling me not to be a hero.

'This gown ain't big enough for the both of us' is a cool thing to say if you're leaving your husband because he keeps wearing your best dress.

You know something bad is about to happen when someone says, 'Hold my beer and watch this.'

'I've got the shoehorn!' – Foot fetishist.

Depresso: When you've run out of coffee.

If you don't buy a ticket, you won't win the EuroMillions jackpot. Also: if you do buy a ticket.

'Daddy, what comes after "U"?' said the little girl doing her homework. 'Usually your mother with a dildo,' said her dad.

I tell you what: if I had a pound for every time I was at one of those parking meters, it would come in very handy.

There have been times that I have known despair. I was crying on the inside. Very dangerous that – you could easily drown.

I can never tell if I'm watching a fireworks display or a spectacular night-time fight between feuding hot-air balloonists.

Why is it important to have plenty of help when changing a light bulb? Many hands make light work.

My new colleagues really take April Fool's Day seriously. Five hours I've been in the office now and they're still all hiding.

The most reliable guide to a man's age is whether he names seagulls George, Steven or Jason.

We had a team-building competition at work. And I won!

Of all the martial arts, karaoke inflicts the most pain.

An escalator can never break – it can only become stairs.

Police arrested two kids yesterday. One was drinking battery acid the other was eating fireworks. They charged one and let the other one off.

'Like father, like son.' – Tarzan, talking about people he likes.

I always know when it's a rude text message because my phone flashes at me.

How do you clear out an Afghani bingo game? Call B52.

Gambling addiction hotlines would do so much better if every fifth caller was a winner.

If Facebook retains ownership of everything you post, I'm going to upload my debt.

You know you're getting old when you have to turn your music down to park your car.

After looking at my bank account, it's time for me to make some tough decisions. Anyone want to buy some Pokemon cards?

I was nearly a step-child. My mother said she would have left me on someone's doorstep if she'd had half a chance.

Story idea: Internet fraudsters hack into my bank account and make a series of shrewd investments. Hilarity ensues.

Never have a tactical wank before sex. Trust me, I learned that the soft way.

I've woken up looking like the episode of *Frasier* where Niles and Daphne finally get together and ruin the entire show forever.

What do Santa and his elves listen to in their Christmas workshop? Wrap music.

You can call it Facebook, but I know scrapbooking when I see it.

My head says 'Swansea', my heart says 'world peace is more than just an impossible dream'. They're thinking about different things again.

If my dad could see me now, he'd be very proud. I'd just want to know why he was in my bedroom.

What's the difference between being hungry and horny? Where you put the cucumber.

What's the difference between a tractor and a giraffe? One has hydraulics, the other has high bollocks.

I'm so good at sleeping I can even do it with my eyes closed.

Why did the chicken go to KFC? To see a chicken strip.

If writers took the 'write what you know' rule seriously, most new novels would be called *Constantly Distracted by the Internet*.

What did one hair say to the other? It takes two to tangle.

What do postal workers do when they're mad? They stamp their feet.

When she asks me 'what do you think?' I think I really should have been listening.

Today is going so slowly my life is flashing before other people's eyes.

What happened to the two ants who got into a fight on a toilet seat? They got pissed off.

I wish there were more TV shows with chefs cooking food to a deadline. That would be nice.

If you spend too much time looking at search engines, you'll go Googly-eyed.

'Always leave them wanting more' is my standard approach to paying bills.

What do you call a man with no legs? Nothing – he might shoot you.

'I love meeting new people.' – Midwife.

Add glamour to your life by saying 'This episode of *I'm An Idiot* was filmed in front of a live studio audience' before leaving the house.

Walked right by an ex-girlfriend today. Not on purpose, I just didn't recognise her with her mouth closed.

I have a weight problem: I can't wait to start eating.

I broke up with my gym. We were just not working out.

Waving a gun around and shouting 'Nobody move!' is a fun way to start a game of Sleeping Lions at a children's party.

What does the winner of the race lose? His breath.

The only reason the railways in Britain print timetables is so that passengers know how late their trains have been.

I took a ring into Cash Converters to sell. The guy said, 'Is this stolen?' I said, 'Of course not.' He said, 'Well, whose finger is this then?'

I was about to put my hand down her knickers when she said, 'You must think I'm a right dirty slapper.' 'Why?' I asked. 'Because you've put condoms on your fingers.'

Why don't robot chickens play basketball? Too many technical fowls.

'He's lovely when you get to know him' is such a nice way of saying, 'Yes, he's a massive idiot.'

You see, I'm against hunting; in fact, I'm a hunt saboteur. I go out the night before and shoot the fox.

How many hipsters does it take to screw in a light bulb? It's a really obscure number; you've probably never heard of it.

Romans called forty 'XL' because that was the age when they had to start buying bigger clothes.

Life is like a box of chocolates. I haven't had one since Christmas.

I always call a spade a spade, until the other night when I stepped on one in the dark.

Fun fact: Every girl pictured in *Nuts* magazine is a member of the National Union of Teachers.

I got into skinny jeans for a little while but I just couldn't pull them off.

Just sending Father's Day cards to the fifty richest men in the world. Has to work one year.

Did you hear about the blind gynaecologist? He could read lips.

Defibrillators repulse me.

Fridge magnets remind me of the time I tried to break into a restaurant but froze with fear at the very last minute.

I've woken up looking like a dream that didn't come true.

Why was six afraid of seven? It wasn't. Numbers are not sentient and thus incapable of feeling fear.

Most children threaten at times to run away from home. This is the only thing that keeps some parents going.

I bought a greyhound about a month ago. A friend of mine said to me, 'What are you going to do with it?' I said, 'I'm going to race it.' He said, 'By the look of it, I think you'll beat it.'

Dishwashers are the Turkish baths of the crockery world: the less you know about what goes on in there, the better.

April showers. I know because I've been spying on her.

The death penalty: Killing people that kill people to show people that killing people is wrong.

Fool me once, shame on you. Fool me twice, shame on me. Fool me three times, shame there's no way to monetise such a great trick.

I always start my diet on the same day ... tomorrow.

1. Buy diary for every year of your life. 2. Leave every page empty. 3. Send to publisher and say it's your autobiography. 4. Cry.

I'm against picketing, but I don't know how to show it.

The average human eats eight spiders while asleep. I sleep with duct tape over my mouth, so somebody's eating my share. Possibly you. Goodnight.

An Olympic event I'd like to see: Synchronised Belly Flopping.

If I eat healthy today then I can have one chocolate as a reward. If I eat unhealthy, I can have the whole box.

I wonder if Chairman Mao constantly thought his cat was calling him.

My ex sent me a picture of her having sex with her new boyfriend. I sent it to her dad.

My favourite form of exercise is running at the first sign of danger.

1. Steal ice-cream van. 2. Drive around slowly but never stop. 3. Be proud to have helped prepare children for life's many disappointments.

You should always be yourself. Unless you discover you're an asshole, son.

Fool me once, shame on you. Fool me twice, shame on you again. And stop picking on me, I'm clearly an idiot.

At the planetarium with my family. I think my wife was surprised to discover she's not the centre of the universe.

Sheryl Crow's song 'Every Day Is a Winding Road' clearly proves she's not a real crow.

What I lack in social skills, I more than make up for in papier-mâché models of people I'd like to be friends with.

Went to the fridge to check my burgers … aaaaannndddd they're off!

I lost a very close friend and drinking partner last week. He got his finger caught in a wedding ring.

Is 8 a.m. too early to remind yourself tomorrow's another day?

The most disapproving of the pharaohs was King Tut.

What do you call a vegetarian crocodile in Egypt? A croc-in-de-Nile.

Just drank two five-hour energy shots. Will I get ten hours of energy? And why is that rainbow giggling at me? And ahhh, my skin is on inside-out!

Whatever you've achieved in life, even the most humble giraffe will look down on you.

If someone says you're acting holier than thou, remind them who used 'thou' in a sentence.

I think, therefore I'm single.

'You're paranoid,' said the doc. 'You're the tenth doctor to tell me that,' I replied. 'You're all in this together, aren't you?'

Don't think less of me for only having £1 to my name. Think less of me for stealing it from the church collection box.

School: 2 + 2 = 4. Homework: 2 + 4 + 2 = 8. Exam: Juan has four apples, his train is seven minutes early, calculate the sun's mass.

What's the difference between a TV and a newspaper? Ever tried swatting a fly with a TV?

I must be good at photography, because my friends always insist that I take all the group photos of them.

The first rule of Fight Club really should have been STOP STARING AT MEATLOAF'S TITS!

I bumped into an old friend the other day. He's got poor eyesight as well.

An invisible man sleeping in your bed, who ya gonna call? Probably the *Sunday Sport*.

What is the difference between anal sex and a microwave? A microwave doesn't brown your meat.

Scientists have found a new family of spiders with front claws. They're not sure what they eat. Anyway, goodnight.

You know that time you said 'Say hello from me!'? Well, I didn't say hello from you.

If someone hid something on page two of Google searches, no one would ever find it.

Show me on the Goo Goo Doll where the '90s touched you.

I just bought an alcoholic ginger beer. He asked for strong lager, but I don't want to encourage him.

Did you hear about how the police were called to a nursery school yesterday? A three-year-old was resisting a rest.

My mate just said, 'What's your favourite mythical creature?' I said, 'Those happy women in Tampax adverts.'

My dog was barking at everyone the other day. Still, what can you expect from a cross-breed?

When someone taps his pockets to check for his wallet, pretend he's on fire and is calmly putting himself out.

What did Arnold Schwarzenegger say about the baritone? It's not a tuba.

Two blondes walk into a building ... you'd think at least one of them would have seen it.

Couples who have been married a long time start finishing each other's sentences. The most popular ending being 'Shut the hell up!'

English football's not dead, though I frequently mourn its passing.

You can tell when you get to Spaghetti Junction because there's a great big fork in the road.

What did one traffic light say to the other traffic light? 'Don't look! I'm changing!'

Why did Billy go out with a prune? Because he couldn't find a date.

Where do bees use the bathroom? At the BP station.

True friends do not judge each other. They judge other people together.

According to population figures, there are 7 billion people on earth compared to only 5 billion twenty years ago. I blame these illegal immigrants.

The Man Who Knew Too Much has died. His family has been informed.

Why don't bunnies make any noise when they have sex? They have cotton balls.

When people accuse me of being pretentious, I simply do what my spiritual forefather Friedrich Nietzsche would do and rise above it.

How many Happy Meals do you need to eat before they start to work? I've just had six and I feel terrible.

Avoid the embarrassment of not knowing which cutlery to use at posh restaurants by never being invited to posh restaurants.

I look so peaceful when my kids are sleeping.

My son said, 'Dad, when you met Mum was it love at first sight?' I said, 'No, second. The first time I didn't know she'd won the lottery.'

Hi, I'm from the government. If you think your problems are bad, just wait till you see our solutions.

I need a punctuation mark that is halfway between a period and an exclamation point so I can answer texts without sounding bored or insane.

It's so sad how some people brush their teeth twice every day and still don't realise they have OCD.

'Knock, knock.' 'Who's there?' 'Doorbell repair man.'

My wife and I have a new arrangement. I can sleep with any woman I want, but she doesn't speak to me or live with me anymore.

A dog is forever in the push-up position.

'Dad, can I go to a 50 Cent concert?' 'Sure son, here's $1, take your sister too.'

Give a man a fish and he'll eat for a day. Teach a man to fish for compliments and he'll say he's leaving Twitter because nobody loves him.

Why don't blind people skydive? It scares the crap out of their dogs.

Archaeologists have just made a new discovery about the Mayan calendar. If you turn it over, there's another 2012 years on the other side.

My mate said, 'My son would like to borrow your *Toy Story* costume.' I said, 'Oh, Woody?'

What's the difference between you and a calendar? A calendar has dates.

Why did the spy stay in bed? Because he was under cover.

Police operator: '999, please hold.' Me: 'OK. Wait, stop stabbing me for a sec.' Murderer: 'OK.'

A great CV should read like a great novel, so always hold back the most startling revelations for the final twenty pages.

Everyone always told me not to run with scissors, but I did. And I now own a large scissors manufacturing company.

If you think the horse burgers in Tesco are bad, wait until you see their unicorn on the cob.

How do you get holy water? Boil the hell out of it.

The only thing worse than being talked about is not being talked about because you took out an injunction to stop people talking about you.

'Sorry, you're overqualified' is such a nice way of saying, 'Hahaha, you're an idiot but we're blaming your degree to make you feel better!'

'The leg bone disconnected from the knee bone, the knee bone disconnected from the thigh bone' – *Mafia: The Musical*.

When people go underwater in movies, I like to hold my breath and see if I would survive in that situation. I died in *Finding Nemo*.

Did you hear about the apartment building that got blown up? Roomers were flying around.

My older sister is tired of me calling her the beta release.

Less love, more sex, no calls, just texts, new boo, no ex, more sleep, no stress.

Did you know you can't even get tapeworms any more? They're all MP3 worms nowadays.

My polo shirt's in mint condition, despite having a hole in the middle.

I have a large seashell collection, which I keep scattered on beaches all over the world.

This jacket potato is seriously overdressed.

Why did the banana split? It saw the ginger snap.

I've always been unlucky. I had a rocking horse once and it died.

I'm not saying my wife's fat ... but I've had to put an energy-saving bulb in the fridge.

What did the calculator say to the maths student? 'You can count on me.'

Headphones, porn and babysitting ... Three things that don't go well together.

They say that alcohol kills slowly. So what? Who's in a hurry?

Do you ever wake up, kiss the person sleeping beside you and feel glad to be alive? I just did and I won't be getting this train again.

What did the judge say to the dentist? 'Do you swear to pull the tooth, the whole tooth and nothing but the tooth?'

Icebergs are actually warm-hearted and kind. Their reputation for coldness stems from that one rogue iceberg ruthlessly sinking the *Titanic*.

I get all my tattoos done for free because I'm an identical twin. I just send my brother back for a refund.

Current relationship status: Prancing around my bedroom to Duran Duran.

When I die, I'm leaving all my debts to charity.

My friend said to me, 'You remind me of a pepper pot.' I said, 'I'll take that as a condiment.'

'I just flew in from New York.' 'Shame, your arms must be tired.'

I swear, the other day I bought a packet of peanuts, and on the packet it said 'May contain nuts'. Well, YES! That's what I bought the buggers for! You'd be annoyed if you opened it and a socket set fell out!

What do tight pants and a cheap hotel have in common? No ballroom.

My parents get on like a house on fire. What began with a tiny spark is now ending in total disaster.

Never think you're better than anyone. Unless you are and they're your boss, in which case tell everyone constantly.

'Talking to you is like pulling teeth' is actually a huge compliment if you're talking to a sadist.

My dispute with a damaged tennis ball is over. Thrown out of court.

Commuters: Liven up the journey home with the simple addition of name tags, bananas, absinthe and Twister.

To be honest with you, I only say 'to be honest with you' when I don't want to be honest with you.

That awkward moment when one twin calls the other twin ugly.

Terrible parenting, a cross-dressing wolf and a brutal axe murder. *Little Red Riding Hood* really is the perfect story for young children.

Giving gum to your friend is like a drug deal: 'You didn't *see* anything, you didn't *hear* anything, and you sure as hell didn't get it from *me*.'

This cold weather is so depressing, can't wait now till the return of summer. Or as it is now affectionately known, 'that Wednesday in June'.

What is the difference between oral and anal sex? Oral sex makes your day and anal sex makes your whole week.

I must be cool because I liked lots of things before they were cool and the fact they never did become cool is irrelevant.

I'm like a fine wine. Always being drunk somewhere.

Dance like nobody's watching the worst dancing in the history of terrible dancing.

You'll finally need me at the end of time.

I hope Crocodile Dundee is now married to the world's tallest woman and goes to weddings and says 'That's not a wife; *this* is a wife!'

I love how the highlights are nearly always the worst part of someone's hair.

Lighten the mood on first dates by playing canned laughter after everything you say.

What do you call a Mexican with no car? Joaquin.

Facebook is for the people you went to school with. Twitter is for the people you wish you went to school with.

I am the author of my life. Unfortunately, I'm writing in pen and I can't erase my mistakes.

Fun fact: If nobody buys you a present or turns up to your party, your birthday is null and void and you stay the same age for another year.

The more I listen to it, the more I think 'Ain't No Mountain High Enough' is the most sinister song ever written.

What's slimy, cold, long and smells like pork? Kermit the Frog's finger.

I'd be so rich now if the eight-year-old me had thought to kidnap that magician who could make money appear from my ear.

'Sometimes I wonder if you even remember what my face looks like,' said my girlfriend's tits.

'What happens in the past should stay in the past!' is a fun thing to say to your credit card company.

The moment when you call and ask to speak to the head idiot and you're put through to your own voice mail.

What day of the week tastes the best? Sunday.

Being right about everything all of the time means never having to say you're sorry.

What's the difference between an outlaw and an in-law? Outlaws are wanted.

It's not the fall that kills you. It's the sudden stop at the end.

Beware of half-truths ... You may get the wrong half.

Every morning: Me: I really can't stay. Bed: But baby, it's cold outside.

The best kinds of laughter: 1. Laughing so hard that your laugh becomes silent. 2. Feeling a six-pack coming. 3. Tears coming out of your eyes.

As a kid I was made to walk the plank. We couldn't afford a dog.

Encourage friends to be more interesting by switching on a Dictaphone and saying 'Idea for a film...' every time they start to speak.

When I'm depressed, I cut myself ... a piece of cake.

When someone hands you a flyer, it's like they're saying, 'Here, you throw this away.'

'I'll be there in five minutes ... If not, read this again.'

Fun fact: Prince is the only child of King Vidor and Queen Latifah.

'You break it, you buy it' ... Oh, hell no. I break it, I leave it and awkwardly walk out.

Imagine being a magician's assistant and not wanting the coffin to be sawn in half at your funeral.

My assistant is out today. Anyone know how to do everything?

My chief contribution to society is being 'the worst-case scenario.'

Leonardo Di Caprio never died in *Titanic*. Last scene: him going underwater. First scene in *Inception*: him waking up on a beach.

I went to a restaurant that serves 'breakfast at any time'. So I ordered French toast during the Renaissance.

People always say I'm really dishy. I have a very round face.

My brain just logged me out due to inactivity and now I can't remember my password.

You've Got Mail is a fun reminder that just fifteen years ago people actually enjoyed reading their emails.

The best thing about telepathy is … I know, right?

Why was everyone so tired on 1 April? They had just finished a March of thirty-one days.

What do you call a cow's mate? Its significant udder.

I tried tap dancing once, but I broke my ankle when I fell into the sink.

'For Christmas, would you like one of those things that tests your blood pressure?' my wife asked. 'You can fuck off if you think your mum's coming for dinner again,' I told her.

What's that Hitchcock film where the middle-aged man falls in love with a mysterious blonde?

I just moped around all weekend. I love mopeds.

Why did Mr Grape leave Mrs Grape? He was tired of raisin kids.

I've got a wife who never misses me. Her aim is perfect.

There are 37,500 search results for 'trivial nonsense' on Google, but just 21,800 on Yahoo.

Fun fact: The song 'Me and Julio down by the Schoolyard' is actually about Ernest and Julio Gallo selling wine to stressed teachers.

'Up there for thinking, down there for dancing,' said the doorman as I decided whether to go to the quiz or the disco.

My mother told me to always be modest. And I am really proud that I am.

Marrying your best friend sounds lovely, except my best friend's an idiot and he's got a girlfriend anyway.

They say shoe size is directly related to penis size. That makes the fear of clowns even worse.

I just want to be as thin as my patience.

A guest bedroom is usually a celebrity bedroom which makes a one-off cameo in your house.

Why did the Irish call their currency the 'Punt'? Because it rhymes with 'bank manager'.

It's impossible to say 'I'll water your plants while you're away' without sounding really creepy.

Two girls were born on the same day, on the same year, to the same parents, but they're not twins: explain. They are triplets.

Avoid getting into trouble for making personal calls at work by not having any friends.

Some people can have all the lights on and still be in the dark.

How can you spot the prostitute at the Miss America pageant? She's wearing a sash that says Idaho.

I can't believe I'd lived this long and still never heard of the 'world-famous pizza' made by the restaurant at the end of my road.

I bet J. R. R. Tolkien's full name is really, really, really long.

Did Jules Verne really write *Around the World in 80 Days*? How long does it usually take to write a book?

Did you know that trampolines used to actually be called jumpolines? That is until 1982, when your mum got on one.

My sister's friend has the strangest looking tits I've ever seen. Wait, disregard that, my binoculars are backwards.

I lose far more sleep than I should worrying about how terrible John Lennon records would be if he were still alive.

My brother and I laugh at how competitive we were as kids. But I laugh more.

The man who invented crosswords has died. May he (4, 2, 5).

Make a carwash more fun by pretending someone ate you and is now getting a vigorous bed bath.

Before somebody visits me, I put a note in my pocket confirming a) it was them who murdered me, and b) why they did it. Just in case.

Halfway through singing a romantic ballad to one of my cats, it occurred to me that I'm going to die alone.

I don't want to be a statistic, unless it's 'Only one man has ever married Scarlett Johansson and won the EuroMillions jackpot on the same day.'

All Jay-Z's problems have been undone by his brother, Ctrl-Z.

If a firefighter's business can go up in smoke, and a plumber's business can go down the drain, can a prostitute get laid off?

Reading a book called *Zero Gravity*. Literally impossible to put down.

I tried to daydream, but my mind kept wandering.

That awkward moment when you ask a lady if she's pregnant and he says no.

The recession has had a detrimental effect on my sex life. It's ages since I've been able to afford it.

I went up into the attic and found a Stradivarius and a Rembrandt. Stradivarius was a terrible painter and Rembrandt made lousy violins.

A bank has been robbed three times by the same bandit. An FBI agent looking for clues interviews one of the bank tellers. 'Have you noticed anything distinctive about the man?' he asks. 'Not really,' replies the teller, 'but each time he turns up he's better dressed.'

A hole has been found in the nudist camp wall. The police are looking into it.

Spoiler alert: You die at the end.

What's black and fuzzy and hangs from the ceiling? A blond electrician.

I can argue my way out of anything, if by anything you mean a previously happy relationship.

'I've been expecting you, Mr Bond.' – James Bond's mother giving birth.

If you love someone, set them free. If they don't come back, call them up later when you're drunk.

History repeats itself because age can be cruel like that.

Turns out company doesn't love misery.

There are two ducks. One duck pulls his pants down. What does the other duck see? His butt-quack.

Holidays got you upset? Just take a deep breath and hold it for twenty minutes.

My thesis on surgical procedure was marked down because the appendix had been removed in error.

My daughter is always taking cucumbers from the kitchen. I'm glad she's promoting a healthy diet.

I just gave my cat some 7UP. Now he's got sixteen lives.

My kids wanted to go caravanning this year. So I've sold them to some gypsies.

I'm wearing socks that hadn't quite dried and wondering if I'm completely out of control.

How do you open the Great Lakes? With the Florida Keys.

Saying 'my whole life has been building up to this moment' is a cool and dramatic way of saying 'I understand the basic concept of time'.

I passed a sign while driving along today, which said 'No u-turn'. So I did an n-turn instead, which actually worked out better for me.

Breaking news: Playboy model found murdered had been very tastefully shot.

If you love someone, tell them. Or just stand outside their house, weeping. Same thing.

I saw a midget prisoner climbing down a wall. As he turned and sneered at me, I thought, 'That's a little condescending.'

A real pedant could find a typo in an empty pocket.

Everything is funny as hell when it's not happening to you.

What do basketball players and babies have in common? They both dribble.

I still remember the first time I had sex – I was terrified. The girl said, 'Have you got any protection?' I said, 'Why? What are you going to do to me?'

Where do computers go to dance? The disk-o.

If you think you aren't creative, buy a gym membership and see how many excuses you find not to use it.

'It never rains…' – North Korean weather presenter.

Step 1: Bought hamster. Step 2: Named it Virginity. Step 3: Lost hamster … Close enough.

Live every day as if it's your blooper reel.

Sometimes I feel as useful as a paramedic at the bottom of the Grand Canyon.

My friend's such an idiot. He just said I was imbecilic, which isn't even a word.

The hardest part of being a shepherd is staying awake while counting your sheep.

I don't burn bridges. I just loosen the bolts a little each day.

I'm going to lose weight. I'm going to exercise every day. I'm going on a diet and I'll stick to it … Hey, is that cake?

After I'd had sex with my girlfriend and lit a cigarette, I felt very guilty. I'd promised my wife I'd never smoke again.

I met the bloke who invented crosswords today. I can't remember his name, it's P something T something R.

Now, I'm not saying you're an idiot. But everyone else is.

I backed a horse last week at ten to one. It came in at quarter past four.

Waitress: Have I kept you waiting long? Me: No, but did you know there are 3,296 squares on the ceiling?

For Sale: 'Everything Must Go!' stickers. Quick sale preferred.

I got stopped by a cop, so I pulled out my 9 millimetre. Once he'd stopped laughing, he arrested me for indecent exposure.

What is at the end of everything? The letter G.

Jim Apple finds introducing himself very problematic when holidaying in France.

I'm very good at remembering random facts. For example, there are 3,500 different types of lice. And that's just off the top of my head.

I accidently had sex with my wife last night, and now she thinks we're friends.

Man rushed to hospital after a sex game went wrong. Doctors found six toy horses in his arse. They described his condition as 'stable'.

Necessity is the mother of Invention. All of my family have very unusual first names.

Yes, it is a banana in my pocket. I'm never pleased to see anyone.

What has four legs but never stands? A chair.

They call me Mr Boombastic. I have no idea why and I've asked them to stop.

Time heals all wounds. As most video game designers will tell you.

I've got to stop saying 'How stupid can you be?' Too many people are taking it as a challenge.

In France, people believe God created the Earth when he was given some lemons and mistakenly made le monde.

The biggest difference between men and women is what comes to mind when the word 'facial' is used.

Commit the perfect murder by hosting a surprise party for someone with a heart condition.

The saddest episode of *Jeremy Kyle* was probably the one in which Thomas Jefferson found out he wasn't the real father of democracy.

He said, 'Your obsession with cats is out of control. I can't handle it anymore.' She cried, 'You're kicking meeeowt?'

If a shark attacks you, DO NOT punch him in the nose. Be the bigger person and just ignore him.

You're always welcome in the 'Show Me' state because Missouri loves company.

'I don't mind people quoting every clever thing I say, but a little credit would be nice.' – Anonymous.

How do Vikings send secret messages? Norse code.

On the ninetieth day of Christmas, my true love said to me, 'You take Christmas too seriously.'

What do you call a king who is only twelve inches tall? A ruler.

I always thought by 2013 we would have flying cars. Instead, we have blankets with sleeves.

Thousands of people quit smoking every year … by dying.

A balanced diet is a biscuit in each hand.

I've had myself waxed 'down there'. Now my socks slide on real easy.

What do lawyers wear in court? Lawsuits.

Moths are really butterflies after they've removed their make-up.

Why was six afraid of seven? Because seven eight nine.

Did you hear about the photographer that got locked in his darkroom? He died of exposure. It was not a pretty picture.

Anyone who says white men can't jump should see me when there's a mouse in the room.

Teacher: Billy, where on the map is the United States? Billy: Over there. Teacher: Right. Now, Susan, who discovered the United States? Susan: Billy!

Fun fact: The thing Meatloaf wouldn't do for love was watch ITV on a Saturday night.

Just finished my review of the national flag of China. Five stars.

What has twelve hands, twelve legs, and twelve eyes? Twelve pirates.

Where does an elephant go when he wants to lie down? Anywhere he pleases.

Women fake orgasms to have relationships. Men fake relationships to have orgasms.

Tying 50,000 helium-filled balloons to your arms is a cool but not entirely foolproof way to make your get-away from a bank robbery.

I'd rather eat my own head than make a ridiculous comparison.

When a man opens the car door for his wife, it's either a new car or a new wife.

What does toast wear to bed? Jammies.

Some lads tried to get into my car last night so I attacked them with a baseball bat. I'm not cut out to be a taxi driver.

So proud that my car is already crawling through traffic at just six months old.

I have a memory like a sieve. I haven't used it since Pancake Day.

I entered a spliff-rolling competition today. Came joint first.

I said to the doctor, 'Every time I close my eyes I see a spinning insect.' The doctor said, 'Don't worry, it's just a bug going round.'

A Buddhist monk approaches a hot-dog stand and says, 'Make me one with everything.'

How can you tell that a train just went by? It left its tracks.

A three-legged dog walks into a saloon in the Old West. He slides up to the bar and announces, 'I'm looking for the man who shot my paw.'

What did the boat say to the pier? 'What's up, dock?'

It is truly easier to forgive your enemies than figure out how to limit their access to your Facebook page.

Twitter is the premature ejaculation of news media.

I like butterflies, I just feel sorry for caterpillars with a fear of flying and no interest in fashion.

My boss says we need a perfect day today, so I'm off to drink sangria in the park, then I'm going to the zoo. Later, a movie too. Then home.

I used to think I had a photographic memory but it never developed.

'Do you actually have friends?' 'Yes! All ten seasons on DVD.'

I don't have a short temper, I just have a quick reaction to bullshit.

Girlfriends are like buses. You wait for ages, and I like the bendy ones best.

I adopted a rescue dog. He rescues food from the table, socks from the laundry, rubbish from the bin and shoes from the wardrobe.

The most confusing American football team ever was the Maltese Falcons.

Memory is what tells a man his wedding anniversary was yesterday.

A daughter asked her mother how to spell 'penis'. Her mother said, 'You should have asked me last night it was on the tip of my tongue.'

What did one elevator say to the other elevator? 'I think I'm coming down with something.'

Sometimes you get news that you just want to shout from the rooftops. Like when my ladder slipped and I got stuck on the roof.

The people who talked about me behind my back discussed me.

My life has been a 'rags to slightly better rags' story.

I hate it when people sit on my imaginary friend Colin, then look at me like I'm the oddball when I complain.

Every day, you should do something that scares you. I leave the house.

Deter burglars by ransacking your own house and pretending to be dead in the hallway.

What is black when clean and white when dirty? A blackboard.

A policeman approached me in the street and said, 'You wouldn't happen to have drugs on you, by any chance?' I replied, 'Sorry mate, I've sold the lot.'

Having a bad day is like watching a boring film – you want to fast-forward to the part where everyone dies.

In Sri Lanka I played with some of the biggest names in world cricket. Warnakulasuriya Patebendige Ushantha Chaminda Vaas. To name just one.

Did you hear about the rabbi who had to circumcise elephants? The pay was terrible but the tips were huge.

'But officer, this *is* my costume. I'm banana nut bread! If I put clothes on, I'm just a normal guy holding a slice of bread.'

Which hand is it better to write with? Neither, it's best to write with a pen.

A dog bit a chunk out of my leg the other day. A friend said, 'Did you put anything on it?' I said, 'No, he liked it as it was.'

I don't have double standards. I have no standards whatsoever.

Fun fact: Every time I sing loudly in the shower, the value of houses in my street drops by 5 per cent.

What do they call the cause of death if an axe fell on you? An axe-i-dent.

How many Vietnam veterans does it take to change a light bulb? YOU DON'T KNOW, MAN, YOU WEREN'T THERE!

I saw my accountant at a strip club and it was really awkward. He pretended not to see me, but his friends slipped a few notes into my thong.

Can't be sure, but I'm looking at the other people on this train and thinking I might be the only one listening to Erasure.

Fun fact: Most action films are made by writing ten random words, changing the font to Webdings and filming the result.

'I went to the dentist this morning.' 'Does your tooth still hurt?' 'I don't know – the dentist kept it.'

People laughed at me when I told them I intended to become a comedian. Well, they're not laughing now.

I'd love to hear your long story. If you can make it short. And interesting.

I always borrow money from a pessimist. He doesn't expect it back.

My brother's a real action man figure. I put him in the loft when I was ten and haven't thought about him since.

Men only want one thing: my best friend's phone number.

Some people are so self-obsessed, like the people on this train who don't want to hear about my day.

Why did Tigger look in the toilet? Because he was looking for Pooh.

Don't worry if you can't remember what happened, Facebook will remember forever.

Last night I was having dinner with Charles Manson, and in the middle of dinner he turned to me and said, 'Is it hot in here, or am I crazy?'

Porn needs to stop making heroes of people who order pizzas they know they're not going to eat. It's so wasteful.

I joined a golf club last week. It kept coming apart.

It's surely no coincidence that Mothering Sunday is nine months after Father's Day.

What kind of balls do dragons play football with? Fireballs.

My son asked about sex. 'Well son, it's like bees. When they poke something, their stinger gets ripped off and they die. Then a bird eats them.'

When someone boasts of juggling their family, career and social life, all I see is the funniest circus act ever.

The worst part of looking at photos of yourself as a five-year-old is realising your hair hasn't been quite as cool since.

Married men live longer than single men, but they're a lot more willing to die.

'Never go back.' – Relationship advice for lit fireworks.

Maybe your mojo doesn't want to be found.

I went window shopping today. I bought four windows.

Why did the hipster go kayaking in a tributary? Rivers are too mainstream.

Arm-wrestling is a nice way to make a friend look tough while holding his hand in public.

I do charity work. I volunteer my opinion just about every day.

After dinner, my wife told me she was expecting a baby. 'You'd better go and open the door,' I said. 'It'll never reach the doorbell.'

There may be no 'I' in 'team', but there are three in 'narcissistic'.

The father of five children had won a toy at a raffle. He called his kids together to ask which one should have the present. 'Who is the most obedient?' he asked. 'Who never talks back to you mother? Who does everything she says?' Five small voices answered in unison. 'OK, Dad, you get the toy.'

It's so sad that the pigeons you see waiting on train platforms don't realise they can fly.

A gorgeous blonde kept on bothering me in the pub last night. She wouldn't even look at me.

I said to my mate, 'I bought my dog a little coat with writing on the back.' He said, 'Oh, what did it say?' I replied, 'Nothing, he's a dog.'

You say you want to bring me back to reality. You're assuming I've been there before.

'Knock, knock.' 'Come in.' 'No, you're meant to say—' 'THIS IS A DISCIPLINARY HEARING, GET IN HERE NOW!'

Turns out, pounding a wooden stake through a vampire's heart works even if the guy's not a vampire.

When were vowels invented? When u and i were born.

You say tomato, I say solanum lycopersicum. No wonder you left me.

Alcohol and calculus don't mix. Never drink and derive.

Why did the tree go to the dentist? It needed a root canal.

I told my girlfriend I had a job in a bowling alley. She said, 'Tenpin?' I said, 'No, permanent.'

When I said I wanted to live life in the fast lane, I didn't mean the one with oncoming traffic.

My girlfriend woke up with a huge smile on her face this morning. I love felt tips.

My friend says I'm childish, but he's just bitter because I always beat him at paper–scissors–stone.

How was the Roman Empire cut in half? With a pair of Caesars.

I wanted the Earth, but then I had a change of heart.

I bought a new Japanese car. I turned on the radio. I don't understand a word they're saying.

Error, no keyboard. Press F1 to continue.

What's the difference between love, true love, and showing off? Spitting, swallowing, and gargling.

Fun fact: Ants date back to 1989, when an all-beetle version of *Honey, I Shrunk the Kids* went disastrously wrong.

Americans eat lots of red meat to help them get irony.

What do you call a camel with three humps? Humphrey.

What kind of car does Mickey Mouse's wife drive? A Minnie van.

The worst part about sharing a name with someone famous is I'm always telling people, no, I'm not *that* Batman.

Whenever I have a Twitter break, I check my job.

I can't believe it. My dog just called me a lying bastard.

'You only live once.' – Pessimistic cat.

I sleep less, I'm tired. I sleep more, I'm tired. Life is impossible.

What do you call a Persian that smokes pot? Harry Potter.

I may look like I'm deep in thought, but 99 per cent of the time I'm just debating what I should eat later.

What do you call a sheep with no head and legs? A fuzz ball.

I got my hair highlighted, because I felt some strands were more important than others.

'This is completely off the record, OK?' – [Name redacted].

'I Just Died in your Arms Tonight' is probably the nicest song ever written by a ghost about a murderer.

Maybe she's born with it, maybe we shouldn't be speculating about hereditary diseases.

What do you call an illegally parked frog? Toad.

'My memory is so bad…' 'How bad is it?' 'How bad is what?'

I got down on one knee and asked her, 'What's it like being so much shorter than me?'

There's a time and a place for everything, with the obvious exception of dogs wearing coats.

The worst part about Friday is when you realise it's only Thursday.

After battling for years to overcome my addiction to alcohol gel, I'm finally clean.

Why are gay men so good at fashion? They've spent so much time in the closet.

If I ever get arrested and I'm allowed one phone call ... I'm calling a locksmith.

A couple are listening to their friends' holiday experiences in the south of England. 'My!' says one. 'We knew you were planning to drive around Kent, but we hadn't realised you were going to take in Surrey, Hampshire and Dorset as well.' 'We hadn't planned to,' says the wife. 'But Ted refuses to ask for directions.'

I honestly enjoy long romantic walks to the fridge.

Money may not solve every problem, but it would likely solve my money problem.

My GPS keeps saying, 'Go back twenty years and enter law school.'

Whoever stole my shoes while I was on that bouncy castle needs to grow up.

I said to my wife, 'Look at this, dear.' I always call her 'dear'. She's got antlers growing out of the side of her head.

I like to think people who leave their umbrellas on trains are optimists who truly believe it will never rain again.

You know you're stressed when you start getting on your own nerves.

Fun fact: I've now buried seventeen rolled-up carpets in my garden to convince my neighbours I'm more interesting than I really am.

My date started choking last night so I quickly pulled my cock out. 'How's that going to help?' asked the waiter.

How does a dog catcher get paid? By the pound.

What has forty feet and sings? The school choir.

A clean desk is a sign of a new employee.

It's a small world, but I wouldn't want to paint it.

'Dad, do you like being married?' 'Sure. Without a wife, I'd never know how to do things the *right* way and I'd still be afraid of death.'

They say that the first black hole was discovered in 1916, but marriage has been around a lot longer than that.

I've been told I'm not ambitious enough. If only there was an Olympic event called 'being a lazy bastard'. That bronze medal would be mine.

I've just eaten an abacus. I believe it's what's inside that counts.

Current relationship status: Waking up next to a half-eaten packet of biscuits.

I can give you the cause of anaphylactic shock in a nutshell.

Weird. My insistence on fifty security questions for every friend to ensure it's not an evil twin is proving a lot less popular than I'd hoped.

I've been shagging this girl from the benefits agency. I am going to abruptly stop without any explanation. See how she likes it.

I read that pigs only sleep on their right side. Which finally explains why I can never get your mum to roll over.

My wife said to me, 'How come I can always smell the scent of another woman on your clothes?' 'Because I'm a fishmonger,' I replied.

I walked into my bedroom last night and caught my wife masturbating with a can of surface cleaner. Mr Muscle, loves the jobs I hate.

What do you call a row of rabbits walking backwards? A receding hare line.

Butterflies may look nice, but never forget they're caterpillar mobsters who ratted out their friends in exchange for new identities.

Why were the early days of history called the Dark Ages? Because there were so many knights.

Getting older is a walk in the park … where no one picks up after the dogs.

What does a dyslexic agnostic insomniac spend most of his time doing? Staying up all night wondering if there really is a dog.

Mind if I borrow your scissors, hammer, and a knife? And a lightsaber if you have it. I've got one of those 'Easy Open' packages here.

Grounded my son for cursing. He turned the girl next door into a frog.

I was woken at three o'clock this morning by my burglar alarm. 'Time to go out robbing,' I yawned.

What do you call an alligator in a vest? Investigator.

Men look at boobs for the same reason women look at puppies in cages. We just want to set them free and play with them.

I told my psychiatrist that everyone hates me. He said I was being ridiculous – everyone hasn't met me yet.

I was going to look for my watch, but I couldn't find the time.

When my mum was in labour, my head got stuck and the midwife had to pull me out. That's how excited I was to see my little brother.

In the DVD commentary *of Fight Club*, they get to the first rule bit and after that it's just a long, awkward silence.

A guy walks into a pub with a lump of asphalt on his shoulder. He says to the barman, 'Give us a pint and one for the road.'

'I love it when things I've written are quoted publicly.' – Me.

Have you ever noticed that anybody driving slower than you is an idiot, and anyone going faster than you is a maniac?

Little Nancy was in the garden filling in a hole when her neighbour peered over the fence. Interested in what the cheeky-faced youngster was up to, he politely asked, 'What are you doing there, Nancy?' 'My goldfish died,' replied Nancy tearfully without looking up, 'and I've just buried him.' The neighbour was very concerned. 'That's an awfully big hole for a goldfish, isn't it?' Nancy patted down the last heap of soil and replied, 'That's because he's inside your cat.'

A man makes a complaint at a cheap hotel. 'My room is swimming in water,' he says. 'Does the roof always leak like that?' 'No sir,' says the receptionist. 'Only when it's raining.'

My small son went with some friends to the local ice rink. When he returned he told me, 'I still don't know if I can skate. I can't seem to stand upright long enough to find out.'

The say you should test your fire alarm once a month. I try, but it's costing me a fortune in houses.

My wife is leaving me because I'm too obsessed with my golf. 'Fine, leave then,' my caddy told her for me.

Prevent slugs invading your home by living in a giant salt mine.

When do cows go to sleep? Pasture bedtime.

Football teams singing the national anthem look like an identity parade to find a mumbling, casually dressed bike thief.

Very proud that so many of my socks have moved on and remarried after the unexpected loss of their partners.

My wife had a go at me last night. She said, 'You'll drive me to my grave.' I had the car out in thirty seconds.

Fun fact: In 1900, only royalty could afford to shop in Poundland.

How do you make a fat girl come? A trail of biscuits.

A vagina is like the weather. Once it's wet, it's time to go inside.

There's no future in time travel.

Arguing with my wife is like getting arrested. Anything you say can and will be used against you.

Today is National Text your Ex Day. So far I've received four 'Hi there, wee cock' and a 'Guess what? I swallow now.' Charming.

Sure, I remember playing doctor as a kid. What I remember most is all the little girls asking me to send them to a specialist.

You see, my next-door neighbour worships exhaust pipes. He's a catholic converter.

If films are a reliable guide, most zombies are killed by a terrible foot injury.

Seriously, don't call yourself a lollipop lady if you're going to react like that when I lick you.

My kids are running around the house shouting 'It's snowing! It's snowing!' I don't care. I'm not letting them in.

What did the lawyer name his daughter? Sue.

Trust me, you'd never eat sausage dogs again if you knew how they were made.

I hate to say I told you so, and that's why I try so hard to be wrong about everything.

Bill Withers singing 'Lovely Day' over and over again sounds like a man trying way too hard to prove he's not having the worst day ever.

Reminder: Adding insult to injury is no longer considered the best way to teach children maths.

Idea for a TV show: Parents are shown a table holding all the money they've ever spent on their child. They then get to choose the money or the child.

Italics are going through a lean spell.

'TGIS!' – Vicars.

Why did the girl throw the butter out the window? She wanted to see a butterfly.

The best part of my dentist visit was him putting me to sleep before extracting my tooth. The worst part was getting home and finding out my boxers were on backwards.

Would it still be considered interrupting if you weren't listening in the first place?

What do you call a fish with no eyes? A fsh.

It's awful how just a few conmen ruined it for the many Nigerian lottery winners who really do want to give money to complete strangers.

He died doing what he loved: skateboarding into volcanoes.

What do you call a young army? Infantry.

Grandparents: Changing the world one forwarded email at a time.

Last night on the way home from the pub, it was a magic carpet. This morning, it's just a doormat I nicked.

Just got on a train without an emergency bottle of water. The spirit of punk lives on.

How do you get tickets to the Tampon 100? Pull some strings.

Where are cars most likely to get flat tyres? At forks in the road.

Unless you fell off the treadmill and smashed your face, nobody wants to hear about your workout.

I love everybody. Some I love to be around. Some I love to avoid. And some I'd love to punch them in the face.

Starting to think everything went wrong the day I sneezed and nobody blessed me.

Dear Board of Education, so are we.

I'm the Jelly Roll Morton of trying too hard to impress people with early twentieth-century jazz references.

I'm so unlucky, I went to the Open University and it was shut.

Does a rabbi charge a lot for circumcisions? No. He just keeps the tips.

Becoming a musician is probably the coolest way of telling people you've lost your job.

There's no greater insult than accusing a genuinely distressed alligator of crying crocodile tears.

What did the wall say when a fish ran into it? Dumb Bass.

My ultimate dream is to tick either 'strongly agree' or 'strongly disagree' on a multiple choice questionnaire.

If my wife doesn't like my cooking she can buy her meth from someone else.

Deep down, I knew scuba diving wasn't for me.

To beat inflation, simply go out and buy a lifetime's supply of everything.

The Four Stages of Going Out: 1. Why do I do this to myself? 2. This isn't so bad 3. We should do this more often! 4. Why do I do this to myself?

I've read this article about OCD 1,375 times and I feel so lucky to not have it myself.

Why couldn't the athlete listen to her music? Because she broke the record.

It always makes me laugh when people ask if I have plans for tonight and I have to point out I don't have a plan for anything.

It turns out standing outside singing 'I wanna be like you-hoo-hoo!' isn't always the best way to be invited to join a private members' club.

I've just learned that tantric sex is where you have sex without moving. I've never tried it myself, but my wife does it all the time.

A diplomat is someone who can tell you to go to hell in such a way that you will look forward to the trip.

A penis is the lightest thing in the world. Even a thought can raise it.

What did the toaster say to the slice of bread? I want you inside me!

What do you call a gangster hobbit? Yolo Swaggins.

Why did the melon jump into the lake? It wanted to be a watermelon.

I love how when you leave dogs in a car on a hot day, they get really excited and try to look out of every window as quickly as possible.

Despite the recent news, Tesco says that their beef burger sales remain stable.

Hear the one about the miscarriage? I overheard it yesterday. The joke was funny but the delivery was all wrong.

'My wife hasn't wanted sex for over a year,' complained my friend down the pub. 'That's just not true, mate,' I replied without thinking.

How many search engine optimisation experts does it take to change a light bulb? Light bulbs buy light bulbs neon lights sex porn.

What makes music on your head? A head band.

An Irishman walks into a bar. He doesn't say anything stupid. Turns out it's Ernest T. S. Walton, winner of the 1951 Nobel Prize in Physics.

The milk of human kindness comes from thinking about udders.

I was in the jungle and there was this monkey with a tin opener. I said, 'You don't need a tin opener to peel a banana.' He said, 'No, this is for the custard.'

Short in the front, long in the back ... Pick-up trucks are the mullets of automobiles.

If I ever have twins, I'll use one for parts.

Ants marching look like the world's smallest funeral cortege. Gets me every time.

You guys are just like family to me. You know, dysfunctional.

What is the difference between a fly and Superman? Superman can fly, but a fly can't Superman.

Why didn't the skeleton go to the party? He had no body to go with.

Scientists say the universe is made up of protons, neutrons and electrons. They forgot to mention morons.

How did the dinosaur pass his exam? With extinction!

I hurt my back the other day. I was playing piggyback with my six-year-old nephew, and I fell off.

Why did the French chef stop working at the haunted restaurant? He got crêped out.

If my house was on fire, I'd pretend the smoke alarm was bleeping out my swearing.

What is the world's longest punctuation mark? The hundred-yard dash.

I didn't hear the sea when I held a shell up. I did, however, get six years in jail for armed robbery of a petrol station.

It's proving very difficult to find a shop selling Left Guard for my other armpit.

I bet the mice under the floorboards at Disneyland are the most resentful mice in the world.

Why does Waldo wear stripes? Because he doesn't want to be spotted.

The wife wanted to try a bit of role reversal in the bedroom. I hated it. I just sat there with my arms folded while she was down the pub.

For years I thought my wife had Tourette's. But apparently she really does want me to fuck off.

What's the difference between a girlfriend and wife? 45 lbs.

Any chameleon that isn't robbing banks on a daily basis is seriously wasting its talent.

I just put £400 in the fruit machine and literally no fruit came out. Fuming.

How does Bob Marley like his doughnuts? Wi' jam in!

'And that's the way the cookie crumbles.' – Final line in the cookie interrogation manual.

My password is WZKAJCM. Those were the letters I had left when a ten-year-old beat me at Scrabble and I will never, ever forget it.

How many Apple users does it take to change a light bulb? None. When the bulb goes, they just replace the house.

'I find these post-it note jokes of yours about my weight problem really distasteful,' my wife said. 'You're not supposed to eat them,' I replied.

It must be awkward being a Cyclops called Iain.

As per his wishes, John requested his favourite team be pall bearers for his coffin. His mum said he always wanted Arsenal to let him down one last time.

Why did the monkey put a piece of steak on his head? He thought he was a griller.

What washes up on small beaches? Microwaves.

What did Tennessee? The same thing Arkansas.

Feel like a movie star by humming the *Psycho* theme to yourself every time somebody murders you in the shower.

Stick a fork in me, I'm kinky.

What's black and white and red all over? A newspaper.

Why can't you play practical jokes on snakes? You can't pull their legs.

Nothing succeeds like a toothless budgie.

What did the teddy bear say when it was offered dessert? 'No, thank you, I'm stuffed.'

I've finally reached the age where I can't function without my glasses ... especially if they're empty.

Odd how all the 'intelligent-life finding instruments' are pointed away from earth...

How do you fix a broken vegetable? With tomato paste.

Dora the Explorer's a bright girl, but parents who let their child go out accompanied only by a monkey should be ashamed of themselves.

Convince people you're a professional hitman by coolly removing your gloves and dropping them in the bin.

What do you call twin policemen? Copies.

Parents: Spelling rather than saying rude words is a good way to ensure your children can spell all the major expletives before they're six.

What did the paper say to the pencil? 'Write on!'

Does it take longer to run from first base to second, or from second to third? From second to third, because there's a shortstop in the middle.

When people cry for help, it's normally just a cry for help.

Why is it OK to kill a cow but the second you have sex with one, it's animal cruelty?

New health study on the psychology of midgets shows that six out of seven dwarfs aren't happy.

Amsterdam is a lot like the Tour de France. It's just a lot of people on drugs riding bikes.

'You complete me.' – Crossword.

Just paying for a mirror at the self-checkout.

What is a tornado's favourite game? Twister.

I wish my wife would stop calling me her 'little cupcake'. The fat cow is really making me nervous.

I like calling the Psychic Hotline and asking them what I'm wearing.

You'd be amazed how unfamiliar the police really are with the whole 'my life, my rules' philosophy.

There's no point robbing Peter to pay Paul. Unless, of course, Peter's a drunk old millionaire and Paul's a bailiff.

I made my eight-month-old son spaghetti bolognese for dinner. To save time, I rubbed the mince in his face and threw the rest on the carpet.

'No more monkeys jumping on the bed'? 'How about you treat my concussed monkey and STOP TELLING US HOW TO LIVE OUR LIVES?!'

'Please God forgive me for the countless murders I will commit in my lifetime.' – Praying mantis.

If my kid couldn't draw, I'd make sure that my kitchen magnets didn't work.

My wife is going to the hairdresser's today. For the next few hours I'll be practising my reaction.

Worry works! Ninety-nine per cent of the things I worry about never happen.

Is Six Degrees of Separation realistic? Asking for a friend of a friend of a friend of a friend of a friend.

What do you call cheese that isn't yours? Nacho cheese.

Why did the man take a pencil to bed? Because he wanted to draw the curtains.

I just made a mental note. It makes no sense whatsoever.

According to the dictionary, a mankini is something mankind should consider beneath it.

I'm terrible at phone sex. Apparently I sound like I'm having a stroke.

Who are the coolest blokes at the hospital? The ultrasound guys.

I went trainspotting once. It was really easy. They're massive and make loads of noise.

What's the difference between three dicks and a joke? Your mum can't take a joke.

My deaf girlfriend told me to fuck off. That's not a good sign.

My doctor said I need to change my lifestyle, so I did ... I robbed a bank and now I'm living it up in Monte Carlo.

No one dies a virgin ... life screws us all.

I try to avoid anything that makes me fat. For example, scales, mirrors...

If you watch Twitter backwards, it's about millions of socially awkward people gradually learning how to survive in the real world.

'Are you sure my balls are supposed to be yellow?' I asked my doctor, dubiously. 'Of course I am,' he said. 'I just potted a red.'

'Doctor, I can't stop singing "The Green, Green Grass of Home".' 'That's the Tom Jones syndrome.' 'Is it common?' 'It's not unusual.'

WiFi and wife? Neighbours have an eye on both of them.

'You say potato, I say potato. We're completely self-obsessed.' – Potatoes.

Karma is like 69. You get what you give.

On the other hand, you have different fingers.

Why is tennis such a loud game? Because each player raises a racket.

The average income of the modern teenager is about 2 a.m.

'Talent borrows, genius steals' is such a great line and I'm so proud that I wrote it.

Who makes the best cake on a baseball team? The batter.

I went to the doctors the other day and I said, 'Have you got anything for wind?' So he gave me a kite.

Using pheromone spray rather than mace helps turn a violent mugging into the start of a beautiful friendship.

Did you hear about the guy who invented 'knock-knock' jokes? He won a no-bell prize.

We have nothing to fear but fear itself. Oh, and snakes, flying, heights, injections and lots of things, actually. Life's terrifying.

I'm not saying it was a bad film, but I watched it for free online and I still feel like I paid too much.

What do you get when you cross an elephant with a kangaroo? Holes all over Australia.

'We need to talk' she said, and I immediately knew what that meant. Our sponsored silence was over.

Roses are red, Facebook is blue, zero mutual friends, who the hell are you?

Flat-pack furniture should be called divorce in a box.

Why did the banker dump his girlfriend? He lost interest.

I had laser eye surgery a few days ago. It didn't work, though. I've been staring at a tin of beans for hours but they're still cold.

It still amazes me that someone once saw a chicken and thought, 'If we chop its head off, pluck the feathers and heat it up a bit, who knows?'

Tom: I bet I can make you say purple. Joe: How? Tom: What colours are in the American flag? Joe: Red, white and blue. Tom: I told you I could make you say red. Joe: You said purple! Tom: I told you I could make you say purple.

'I'm very much a people person.' – Slave trader.

What should you do if a condom splits? The same.

When bees visit the same flower over and over again, it's called stalking.

What do an alcoholic and a necrophiliac have in common? They both like to crack open a cold one.

'I love Eminem!' 'I like Skittles better.' 'No, the rapper you idiot.' 'You're the idiot. What's so good about an M&M wrapper?'

The guy who invented applause must have looked like an idiot when he first tried it out.

Don't be so smug, young people. One day you too will wake up and not recognise anyone on the cover of *People* magazine.

What would you call a humorous knee? Fun-ny!

Malaria kills far more people than plane crashes, so never try to save money on air travel by hitching a lift with a mosquito.

The corkscrew's the only bit of my Swiss Army knife I've ever used, if you're wondering how long I'd survive in the wild.

What did the picture say to the wall? 'I've been framed.'

What do you get when you cross a parrot and a lion? I don't know, but when it talks you'd better listen.

'I'm so empty inside.' – This wine bottle. Also, me.

Why did the gardener plant his money? He wanted his soil to be rich.

In the future, every dog will be famous for 105 minutes.

'We just get too attached to people.' – Lonely earrings.

My wife says I have a preoccupation with vengeance. We'll see about that.

Phones get thinner and smarter. People get fatter and stupider.

A good friend of mine drowned. So at the funeral we got him a wreath in the shape of a lifebelt. It's what he would have wanted.

Scuba diving lessons: See below for details.

I would go the extra mile for you … in the opposite direction.

Smartphone owners: That blurred bit just off the edge of the screen is called life.

The good thing about marriage is that you can have sex at any time you want. As long as you're the one with the vagina.

I love a good pop song, but if Lionel Richie tried dancing on the ceiling all night long in my house, I'd be absolutely fuming.

What does a perverted frog say? Rubbit.

Idea for a TV show: *When the Saints Go Marching in.* Ecclesiastical bailiffs reclaim Bibles from people who haven't paid for their sins.

I can usually tell within 100 years of meeting someone if they're going to be a lifelong friend.

When I was a kid I used to pray every night for a new bike. Then I realised that the Lord doesn't work that way, so I stole one and asked him to forgive me.

Fun fact: Mr T's surname is Tulips.

Honey, do you have anything you'd like to say before football season starts?

A deck of cards is a fun reminder that members of the royal family are just a little bit better than everyone else.

Of course I talk to myself ... Sometimes I need expert advice.

I can do a fairly good impression of someone who cares about your problem.

How many therapists does it take to change a light bulb? Just one, but the light bulb has to want to change.

My wife asked me which Polynesian island states to avoid on her folk music tour. I said, 'Skip Tuvalu, my darling.'

Yesterday, all my troubles seemed so far away. Today I have a dreadful hangover.

My wife and I were fighting like hammer and tongs. She won, she had the hammer.

I was working in Subway when a Greek girl came in and said, 'Do you have any feta cheese?' I replied, 'I'm quite into gimp masks and fisting.'

What do you call a Russian with Tourette's Syndrome? Yukanol Fukov.

Airport: A place where the distance to your gate is inversely proportional to the time available to catch your flight.

What did Sean Connery say when a book fell on his head? 'I have only my shelf to blame.'

Just reported a zookeeper for completely ignoring the 'Do Not Feed the Animals' sign.

I've just won the 'Most secretive person 2013' award. I can't tell you how much it means to me.

What do you call a gorilla with a banana in each ear? Anything you like. He can't hear you.

What's the difference between light and hard? You can go to sleep with a light on.

'I think we should just be friends' is such a nice way of saying 'I never want to see you ever again.'

Why did the orange stop in the middle of the hill? It ran out of juice.

Octogenarians must hate that veterinarians are fully qualified after just five years.

The best part of being a lonely goldfish is that no one can tell you're crying and even you will soon forget why.

A salesman knocked on my door today. 'Who currently provides your internet?' he asked. I said, 'My next-door neighbour.'

How do you find a blind man on a nude beach? It isn't hard.

Why did the Mafia cross the road? Forget about it.

The name's Bond. James Bond. James Bartholomew Reginald Bond. Just call me Bond.

'Knock, knock.' [Silence] 'Knock, knock.' [Silence] 'Knock, knock.' [No joke, I'm hiding under the bed, the bailiffs are here.]

Sadly, the airport's X-ray machine revealed a slight tear and my suitcase will now require stitches.

I just saw a chicken crossing the road. Poultry in motion.

Just found out the human-shaped chalk outlines on my street aren't landing pads for expert skydivers. Awful.

What do you call a nun in a wheelchair? Virgin Mobile.

I celebrated Thanksgiving in an old-fashioned way. I invited everyone in my neighbourhood to my house, we had an enormous feast, and then I killed them and took their land.

Why can't T-Rexes clap? Because they're dead.

What goes under your feet and over your head? A skipping rope.

My boss is like a father to me: constantly disappointed.

What occurs once in a month, twice in a moment but never in a day? The letter M.

There's a very thin line between a misunderstood genius and a pretentious idiot nobody likes.

What did Delaware? A New Jersey.

Why did Cinderella get kicked off the football team? Because she ran away from the ball.

How do you get an eighty-year-old woman to yell 'fuck'? You get another eighty-year-old woman right next to her to yell, 'Bingo!'

Déjà Moo: The feeling that you've heard this bullshit before

Where do you go to find a million-story building? The library.

Another World's Oldest Man has died. This is beginning to look suspicious.

Business idea: A home surgery kit called Suture Self.

One day my father took me aside and left me there.

When I was young, I had to walk all the way to the TV to change the channels.

Relationships are a lot like algebra ... Ever looked at your X and wondered Y?

Did you hear about those new corduroy pillowcases? They're making lots of headlines.

It's not you, it's me. Hahaha, not really – it's 100 per cent you. Nothing's ever my fault.

Why did the cucumber call 999? It was in a pickle.

Weight Watchers is a not-for-profiteroles organisation.

Tonight I'm going to have my favourite drink. It's called 'a lot'.

You can achieve everything you want if you're unambitious enough.

'The pen is mightier than the sword.' – Naïve samurai's last words.

Undress for the job you want, not the one you have.

Optimism: Where there's a will, there's a way. Pessimism: Where there's a will, someone died.

Singer Neil Diamond started his career as Neil Coal. He changed his name when the pressure got to him.

'You can't taste me, until you undress me.' – Banana.

Warning: Making aeroplane noises while feeding your children can give them a very misleading idea of the tastiness of aeroplanes.

First you're telling me to be myself, then you're telling me to stop being an idiot. Make your mind up.

I had a wonderful dream last night. I dreamed that Brigitte Bardot came up to me and said, 'I will grant you three wishes. Now what are the other two?'

What do you call a girl that raps about women rights? Feminem.

It's so sad that swans are associated with arm-breaking just because that one swan was owed money and resorted to violence to get it.

I watched my first silent movie the other day. The wife wasn't there.

The more I look at my Swiss Army knife, the more I understand why the Swiss Army never gets involved in wars.

It's not really my wife's fault she's fat. She's an omnomnomnivore.

In most cases, a lack of self-awareness is a blessing.

What does a 75-year-old woman have between her breasts that a 25-year-old doesn't? Her navel.

This match won't light. Which is weird, because it did this morning.

What's black and white and red all over? An embarrassed mime.

Sadly, most alcoholic drinks refuse to admit they have a problem.

After a fight, a man said to his wife, 'You know, I was a fool when I married you.' She replied, 'Yes, dear, but I was in love and didn't notice.'

'I have a bullet with your name on it,' I said to my wife. 'And it has seven different vibration levels.'

I can't help being lazy. It walks in the family.

Why don't North Koreans go to heaven? Because they have no Seoul.

A comprehensive search found precisely zero hot singles in my area, and now I'm wondering how many other lies the internet has told me.

My friend drank a bottle of furniture polish. Came to a nasty end but had a beautiful finish.

Don't worry about what people think. They don't do it very often.

I bought a £7 pen because I always lose pens and I got sick of not caring.

Seriously, why bother learning to use Photoshop if you're *not* planning an elaborate lie involving yourself and the entire cast of *Mad Men*?

I will not keep calm or carry anything.

How do you stop millions of children from going to bed hungry every night? Take away their beds.

I ordered a leather sofa off the Ikea website last week. They sent me a dead cow and some instructions on how to skin it.

The recipe said 'set the oven to 180 degrees', so I did, but now I can't open it because the door faces the wall.

'My wife's gone to the Caribbean.' 'Jamaica?' 'I DON'T KNOW WHERE SHE IS, SHE'S LEFT ME. THE HOLIDAY STORY'S A TRAGIC LIE.'

What's the difference between a porcupine and a Hummer? The porcupine has the pricks on the outside.

My husband asked me to dress up as a nurse tonight to fulfil his fantasy … that we have health insurance.

Where do you learn to make banana splits? In sundae school.

I only found out how much my father despised me when he died and left all his money to the local cats' home. He hated cats.

A bear drops an e and turns into a bar. Bear: Er … just a water, please. Barman: Why the big pause? Bear: I love you, man.

I wonder how police on bicycles arrest people … 'All right, get in the basket.'

I went into a hairdresser's that charged £45 for a cut. As I sat down in the chair the woman asked, 'How much do you want off?' '£35,' I replied.

I think my girlfriend's frigid. She's Swedish, and I didn't really pay attention to her name.

My parents want to retire somewhere hot and expensive, so I'm putting them in a care home.

Make jury service fun by dressing up as a different notorious criminal every day.

The worst thing about being kidnapped would probably be the embarrassing lack of facial hair when I was released.

Current relationship status: Booking flights just to get frisked at the airport.

I've just had an email from Screwfix – apparently they're not a dating agency.

Lawyers are like rhinoceroses; thick skinned, short sighted and always ready to charge.

'To pre-empt your questions!' 'What do we want?' 'Now!' 'When do we want it?'

When is a car not a car? When it turns into a garage.

I'm pretty sure God is a man. Because whoever put this crazy world together obviously didn't follow the instructions.

The Church of England is to compete against Wonga with payday loans. Since Jesus managed to feed the 5,000 with a few loaves and fish, I'm sure He will have no problem turning a £100 loan into a £3,237,982.45 debt.

I have a love–hate relationship with mood swings.

What do you guys think of message boards? I'm all forum.

The story of Mr Bump is far less amusing when you realise he's just a tragic drunk.

Hold that pose. My camera is ringing.

When the doctor told me that he'd botched my operation, my heart was in my mouth.

I'm sorry I got angry and said a lot of things I meant but shouldn't have said.

I've owned three golden retrievers and not once has one of them brought me any gold.

Bargain hunting is the most brutal of all blood sports.

If my memory gets any worse I'll be able to plan my own surprise party.

It makes sense why women hate premature ejaculation so much. Our whole lives we're taught that nothing worth having comes easy.

The other night I had an argument with my wife in the launderette but we went home and ironed things out.

Your threats mean nothing, armed robber telling me not to be a hero. I've already fainted.

If you think nobody cares if you're alive, try missing a couple of payments.

I can only imagine how I'd look in a blindfold.

After my girlfriend told me she was pregnant I started thinking about names. In the end I went for Juan Carlos and got on the next flight to Spain.

It's so sad how that one guy managed to ruin the reputations of all the perfectly civilised men from Nantucket.

I see nothing but continued growth and expansion for the foreseeable future ... but enough about my diet.

Keep your head high and your middle finger higher.

What's the difference between an arts student and a table? A table can support itself.

Remembering all the people who said I was too lazy to achieve anything in life is what gets me out of bed in the afternoon.

A Roman walks into a bar, holds up two fingers, and says, 'Five beers, please.'

How did the butcher introduce his wife? 'Meet Patty.'

The definition of insanity is doing the same thing over and over again while surrounded by papier-mâché models of your ex-girlfriends.

I could be a morning person. If morning happened around noon.

Just seems wrong that typing 'a Googlewhack' into Google gets 74,000 results.

What do the Starship Enterprise and toilet paper have in common? They both circle Uranus looking for Klingons.

Lazy People Fact #5812672794: You were too lazy to read that number.

'There's plenty of fish in the sea…' 'That's cool and all, but I'm human.'

What do you call a potato wearing glasses? A spectator.

My parents think I've made nothing of my life. My Tamagotchi is sixteen years old. You do the maths.

If the Mayans have taught us anything, it is that if you don't finish something, it's not the end of the world.

'There's a sleeping person. Let's go ask it questions.' – Children.

My nephew just asked if I had a street name and I said Clifton Terrace, and why is he laughing?

My neighbour John was on his deathbed and gasped pitifully, 'Give me one last request, dear.' 'Of course, John,' his wife said softly. 'After I die,' he said, 'I want you to marry Bob.' 'But I thought you hated Bob,' she said. With his last breath John said, 'I do!'

I've said it before and I'll say it again. 'It.'

Fool me once and I will leave you immediately. I'm VERY sensitive.

Why can't you hear a psychiatrist using the bathroom? Because the 'p' is silent.

I always stop to help women who have broken down on the road. I don't know shit about cars, but I do know how good porn starts off.

Take my advice – I'm not using it.

The depressing thing about tennis is that no matter how good I get, I'll never be as good as a wall.

My girlfriend was giving me head. She said, 'Let me know when you're close.' Then she hung up on her husband and carried on sucking me off.

I read an actual newspaper today! For those of you who don't understand, a newspaper is like the internet but made of paper.

My uncle took my nose in 1978. He still has it.

How did you get a fat girl into bed? Piece of cake.

Imagine getting to the end of a day and not regretting literally everything you'd done.

I've been left to my own devices. Now wishing I had better devices.

Four fonts walk into a bar the barman says 'Oi, get out! We don't want your type in here.'

I decided to put laxatives in my hash brownies just for shits and giggles.

Where do cars go for a swim? At the carpool.

Girl: Hey, what's up? Boy: If I tell you, will you sit on it?

The best time to give advice to children is while they're young enough to believe you know what you're talking about.

What did the melon tell her boyfriend when he proposed? 'Yes, but we cantaloupe.'

Avoid looking too keen by never speaking to anyone.

Lite: The new way to spell 'light', now with 20 per cent fewer letters!

One, three, five, seven, nine and eleven kicked the holy shit out of two and four. Two and four did not stand a chance because they were fighting against the odds.

I can't believe my life coach is planning to sell me in the January transfer window.

I found a way to combine Oxo cubes with yeast, so now my stock is rising.

Porn is so unrealistic – there's no way they'd be doing THAT on brand-new sofas.

I like a good long cuddle with my girlfriend after sex. It's the quickest way to deflate her.

I've just been accused of being 'a plagiarist'! Their words, not mine.

I don't like my hands. I always keep them at arm's length.

Why would Snow White make a great judge? She was the fairest in the land.

1. Visit pub in disguise. 2. Show barman photo of yourself and ask if he's seen you. 3. Go back later without disguise. 4. Enjoy mystery man status.

Reminder: If you're doing more than 90 per cent of the work, it's not a cuddle.

What's a pirate's favourite letter? You'd think it would be the arrr but it's really the sea.

I'm still waiting for 'Bring Your Brain to Work Day'.

Do pyromaniacs wear blazers?

Turns out a family changing room *isn't* a place you can go if you want to change your family for a different one.

When my horny secretary came in crying because she'd just split up with her boyfriend, I thought I'd take advantage of her. So I put her on minimum wage.

'So much to get angry about, so little time.' – Twitter.

'Every man wants to marry a female version of himself.' – Penguins.

A man stole hundreds of pounds' worth of stock from Odeon. Police are asking locals to report anyone seen with a Coke and a bag of Minstrels.

Where does a boat go when it is sick? To the dock.

I hate people who say 'age is just a number' – age is clearly a word.

If I could choose, being eaten by lions while David Attenborough narrates would be my ideal way to go.

You can't have everything. Where would you put it?

It's amazing to think how different your life might be if you'd done literally everything completely differently.

Nothing sadder than preparing your 'Ooh, a surprise party, for me?!' face, walking into a room and just finding the cat looking a bit cross.

The worst part about being a giraffe is having a lot of time to think about your mistakes when you're sinking into quicksand.

I'm not saying my wife's fat, but I've had to put all the chocolate biscuits well out of reach. On the floor.

I came from a very poor family of five children. We all used to sleep in the same bed. I never slept alone until I got married.

How many emo kids does it take to screw in a light bulb? None, they all sit in the dark and cry.

My alarm clock has a secret track where if I leave it ringing long enough I can hear my flatmate calling me an idiot.

Not to be competitive, but I am an excellent sleeper.

I tried to fight fire with fire, and then I remembered that firemen usually use water.

'Don't try this at home' OK, I'll try it at my friend's place.

I love how people say they're 'expecting' a baby, as though it might be something else, like a penguin.

I'm so ugly, when I wank I pretend I'm somebody else.

Broccoli: I look like a tree. Walnut: I look like a brain. Mushroom: I look like an umbrella. Banana: Guys, change the topic.

Apparently, I offended my optician last week. She saw me out in town and waved at me, but I didn't notice her. Well, whose fault is that?

Sometimes, when I don't want my girlfriend to find something, I put it in her purse.

My friend keeps telling me to stop impersonating butter. I can't, I'm on a roll now.

Watching a film with subtitles is like being told off by someone you're too scared to look in the eye.

What did the stamp say to the envelope? 'Stick with me and we will go places.'

The Karate Kid is my favourite film about a young person taking advice from an old person, as if that would ever happen.

All the king's horses and all the king's men considered putting Humpty together again a woeful misuse of their time and resources.

I knew my wife was horny the moment I ripped her knickers off, threw them against the wall and they stuck.

A new employee is called into the personnel manager's office. 'What's the meaning of this?' asks the manager. 'When you applied for the job you told us you had five years' experience. Now we discover that this is the first job you've ever had.' 'Yes,' replies the young man, 'but your ad also said you wanted somebody with imagination.'

A young man goes for a job interview and is asked what sort of employment package he expects. 'What I expect is a starting salary of £30,000 a year, six weeks' annual holiday and a Jaguar for a company car.' 'All right,' says the interviewer. 'How about this? We pay you £40,000 a year, rising to £60,000 after two years. You get eight weeks' annual leave, your own secretary and PA, and we'll promote you to board level after four years.' 'Wow!' says the young man. 'You've got to be joking!' 'I am,' replies the interviewer. 'But you started it.'

A guest speaker was talking to a member of the audience after his rather long speech. 'How did you find my speech?' 'Oh, very refreshing, very refreshing indeed.' 'Did you really?' asked the delighted speaker. 'Oh yes. I felt like a new person when I woke up!'

Welcome to Pessimists Anonymous. Sorry there aren't any chairs, we weren't expecting anyone to come.

The bathroom scale seems to be taking a while to load. I may be over capacity.

I slept like a log last night. I woke up in a fireplace.

Two silkworms had a race. It ended in a tie.

If there's something strange in your neighbourhood, who ya gonna call? Probably the police.

Why was the baseball player arrested in the middle of the game? He was caught stealing second base.

Charlie and the Chocolate Factory is my favourite book about a weird guy who murders four children then convinces another to live with him.

There was a man in prison, and he tried to find a way out, but he couldn't. Finally, he tunnelled his way out and ended up in a park. He shouted, 'I'm free! I'm free!' A little girl replied, 'Cool, I'm four.'

My new book, *Publishers Are Idiots*, is proving far less popular with publishers than I'd hoped.

What do you call a boat that gives fresh breath? A shipmint.

What's the difference between love and herpes? Love doesn't last forever.

Give up now to avoid disappointment in the future.

My mum walked in my room and said, 'You'll go blind if you do that.' I was so embarrassed I dropped my binoculars and missed the eclipse.

My doctor says I have a cute tinnitus. Bit inappropriate and I'd rather he just cured the ringing in my ears.

I had a dream last night that I was cutting carrots with the Grim Reaper. I was dicing with death.

Did you hear about the murder mystery porno? In the end, everyone did it.

You have to question the modus operandi of people who use Latin for no reason.

My girlfriend hates it when I sneak up on her. According to her lawyer, she also hates it when I call her my girlfriend.

The awkward moment when your parents don't appreciate the hilarious child they have been blessed with.

I've given hundreds of orphans a new home, if eating jelly babies counts.

The cool part about naming your kid is that you don't have to add six numbers to make sure the name is available.

Why did the traffic light turn red? You'd turn red too if you had to change in the street.

It's awkward touching hands with a woman in a popcorn bag. Especially if you don't know her and she doesn't know you're eating her popcorn.

A bitter shandy is one that can't forgive you for pouring lemonade on its head.

A man wakes up in hospital. The doctor says, 'There's good news and bad news.' The man says, 'Tell me the bad news first.' The doctor says, 'We amputated your left leg, and tomorrow we will amputate the other leg.' The man grew very sad and asked, 'What's the good news?' The doctor says, 'See that guy over there? He wants to buy your shoes.'

How do you apply for a job at Hooters? They just give you a bra and say, 'Here, fill this out.'

Lottery winners receive their cheque in Rich Text Format.

It's so sad that hands are twins and the stupid one has to watch as the clever one gets all the important jobs.

The success of your criminal career is measured by the number of times the word 'Attempted' appears on your record.

When you say things can only get better, you're seriously underestimating my ability to make things much, much worse.

We should have a way of telling people their breath stinks without hurting their feelings like: 'Well, I'm bored, let's go brush our teeth.'

The first rule of OCD club is that there must be a second rule, so we have an even number of rules.

Two cows are standing next to each other in a field. Daisy says to Dolly, 'I was artificially inseminated this morning.' 'I don't believe you,' said Dolly. 'It's true, straight up, no bull!'

How do colour-blind people see porn? In fifty shades of grey.

'Dad, why don't people make snowwomen?' 'Because snow isn't cold enough … Don't tell your mum.'

Algebra rule: If it seems easy, you're doing it wrong.

My wife said to me, 'Laugh at your problems. Everyone else does.'

Who can hold up a bus with one hand? A crossing guard.

'Army chief says cuts could be dangerous.' Let's hope nobody tells him about guns and bombs.

The best nicknames are usually the ones people don't know they have.

It would be a lot easier to be a hard worker if my company didn't block access to porn sites on the internet.

The wife and I were dirty texting earlier when she said, 'You can stick it anywhere tonight.' So I shagged her sister.

What is it that even the most careful person overlooks? Her nose.

My mate said, 'It must be awful for you having a surname like Depressant.' I said, 'It's a lot worse for my Auntie.'

The fact that jellyfish have survived for 650 million years despite not having brains is great news for stupid people.

When you're being chased by a large swarm of bees, it's of little consolation that so many of them are just following the crowd.

Seriously, whoever invented petting zoos belongs in prison.

Skype conversations: 5 per cent 'Hey, how are you?' 95 per cent 'CAN YOU HEAR ME?!'

You are what you eat, and I wish I'd never eaten that bumbling idiot.

Why do I have a superiority complex? I'd be happy to explain, but I doubt you'd understand.

What is the musical part of a snake? The scales.

How do you know if a restaurant has a clown as a chef? When the food tastes funny.

What do you get when you mix LSD and birth control? A trip without the kids.

What do you call a black man selling drugs? A pharmacist, you racist.

How do you cure a headache? Put your head through a window and the pane will just disappear.

Encourage greater efficiency and promote family values at the same time by holding Bring Your Child to Work Day at the weekend.

What's the best part of gardening? Getting down and dirty with my hoes.

What do you give a lemon in distress? Lemonade.

The onions aren't making me cry. It's just being in the kitchen in general.

Dear Santa, this Christmas I'd like a fat bank account and a slim body. And please don't mix up the two like you did last year.

My ghost writer is dead to me.

If it wasn't for Twitter, we'd all be on Facebook refreshing our pages every five minutes, wishing for new notifications.

I got a parrot and it talked, but it didn't say 'I'm hungry', so it died.

I went to Switzerland for an assisted suicide. I arrived just in time for the welcome breakfast ... The sick bastards were serving Cheerios!

'Do you sell magazines?' I asked the assistant in W. H. Smith. 'Of course we do,' she said, rolling her eyes. 'Great! Fill this up,' I said, placing my AK-47 on the counter.

I've got a friend who's fallen in love with two school bags. He's bi-satchel.

Save money on your home and contents insurance by never buying a home or any contents.

A shepherd once told me to count his thirty-seven sheep and then round them up. So I told him there were forty.

Two hydrogen atoms walk into a bar. One says, 'I think I've lost an electron.' The other says, 'Are you sure?' The first says, 'Yes, I'm positive.'

I told my wife I was leaving her. 'Is it because I make fun of your little willy?' she laughed. 'No,' I replied. 'I've just never been that into you.'

1. Find girl. 2. Place metal detector on her left breast. 3. Say you're looking for someone with a heart of gold. 4. Laugh and later marry.

What animal has two grey feet and two brown feet? An elephant with diarrhoea.

I find adverts very persuasive. They persuade me to switch channels immediately.

Considering they have the biggest brains in the world, whales have written surprisingly few great novels.

I opened up a bottle of Coke and it said, 'Sorry, you didn't win.' I didn't even know I was playing, yet I was still disappointed.

Every time my wife takes the car out, she comes back with the same question: 'Guess who I ran into?'

I never drive around with my payslip in my car. Should I die in an accident, I don't want people to assume it was suicide.

I'm trying to imagine a world where everybody *didn't* love Raymond, but it's just too horrific.

I have three heads, five legs, seven arms and 444 fingers. What am I? A liar.

Why don't honest people need beds? They don't lie.

It would be so sad if your dream was to sweep the board at the Oscars and you had to take a cleaning job sweeping the boards at the Oscars.

I under-think everything.

A photon checks into a hotel and the porter asks him if he has any luggage. The photon replies, 'No, I'm travelling light.'

What's the difference between a pregnant woman and a light bulb? You can unscrew a light bulb.

Listen, calling people names says a lot more about you than it does about them, you idiot.

1. Set off airport metal detector. 2. Say you have a lot of iron in your diet. 3. Laugh all the way to the interrogation room.

Shakespeare: To be or not to be. Sartre: To do is to be. Socrates: To be is to do. Scooby Doo: Do be do be do.

What did one wall say to the other? 'I'll meet you at the corner.'

I wish I had parents like Dora's. They let her go everywhere.

A guy goes to the store to buy condoms. 'Do you want a bag?' the cashier asks. 'No,' the guy says. 'She's not that ugly.'

As chairman of the Blind Society, I was accused of needlessly wasting money. So I arranged a fireworks display to cheer everyone up.

Here's what I don't get about Spiderman. Why haven't any of his arch enemies just squashed him with a giant shoe?

Why did the cow jump over the moon? Because the farmer had cold hands.

The recruitment consultant asked me, 'What do you think of voluntary work?' I said, 'I wouldn't do it if you paid me.'

Why did the boy take a ruler to bed? To see how long he slept.

What did the painter say to the wall? 'I got you covered.'

Trust me, you don't get to be the fifty-third most senior person in a sixty-person company without making a few enemies.

Why do you never tease a fat girl with a lisp? Because she's thick and tired of it.

My wife said, 'I think we should do something really scary for the kids this Hallowe'en.' I said, 'We could take them to your mother's.'

I wish there was a rollover plan for childhood naps I refused to take.

My wife does really good bird imitations. She watches me like a hawk.

It's so sad that Charlie lacked Willy Wonka's entrepreneurial spirit and bankrupted the chocolate factory within six months.

I just want people to love me for who I am *before* I start drinking tequila.

You'll never believe what my imaginary friend just did.

Someone should invent an alarm clock that automatically reports you sick when you've pressed snooze three times.

I sympathise with sharks because if my house flooded and some idiot turned up on a surfboard, I'd be furious too.

Scones are just biscuits that studied abroad.

There are no limits to what you can accomplish when you're supposed to be doing something else.

I had a fight with my wife last night. She asked me what was on the TV and I said, 'Dust.'

Film fact: *Paperman* is better than *The Rock*, but not as good as *Edward Scissorhands*.

Why don't traffic lights ever go swimming? Because they take too long to change.

Can you say 'Richard and Robert had a rabbit' without using the 'r' sound? Sure, Dick and Bob had a bunny.

My girlfriend has this weird, sick, demented sexual fetish. Cuddling.

What type of music are balloons scared of? Pop music.

If you've ever wanted to be a fly on the wall *anywhere*, you really need to buck your ideas up and show more ambition.

Whoever said 'Don't cry over spilt milk' hasn't seen the price of food lately.

'Do not stand at my grave and weep. I am not there, I do not sleep.' – Spilt Milk, the poetry years.

Why did Mozart get rid of his chickens? They kept saying 'Bach, Bach.'

'What do we want?' 'New joke formats!' 'When do we want—' 'SHUT UP!'

When I was in the scouts, the leader told me to pitch a tent. I couldn't find any pitch, so I used creosote.

When it comes to advice, I'm a giver.

If you trip over in public, a cool thing to do is break into a jog, leave the country, have plastic surgery and change your name.

This policeman came up to me with a pencil and a piece of very thin paper. He said, 'I want you to trace someone for me.'

My gangster wife was insistent that I use her massive bum for shoplifting hats. So I popped a cap in her ass.

I have an on/off relationship with trains.

Never mind gift horses, I rarely look anyone in the mouth. It's weird.

Apparently my first word was 'Dada', after which I never mentioned avant-garde art movements ever again.

My spiritual home has been repossessed.

Knock, knock. Who's there? Biggish. Biggish who? No thanks, not today.

I'm on a thirty-day diet. So far I've lost ten days.

What do you call a scared train? A fright train.

Just got back from the hospital. They reckon I might have pneumonoultramicroscopicsilicovolcanoscoliosis, but at the moment it's difficult to say.

Spooning: For girls – cute, warm and straight to sleep. For boys – face full of hair, make-up all over new top, dead arm and an awkward boner.

How do you invite a native Alaskan to your home? You Eskimover.

Avoid public humiliation by never leaving the house.

A conscientious porn star is always hard at work.

Just so you know, 'Who's your favourite Miss Marple?' is a far less successful chat-up line than it should be.

What is the difference between snowmen and snow-women? Snowballs.

If you're thinking of making a joke about Self-Harm Awareness Day, bite your tongue.

Sorry for punching you in the face, but you should've told me that was an oatmeal raisin cookie and not chocolate chip before I bit into it.

I'm just a boy, standing in front of a girl, wishing she'd stop moaning about tall people and enjoy the concert.

I'm starting to think my birthday suit doesn't even like birthdays.

I'll tell you what I love doing more than anything: trying to pack myself in a small suitcase. I can hardly contain myself.

What's the slipperiest country in the world? Greece.

The fact that guests on *Desert Island Discs* never choose a record player as their luxury item shows just how silly celebrities can be.

What kind of bees produce milk? Boobies.

Why does Dr Pepper come in a bottle? Because his wife divorced him.

My boss told me, 'You're not smart enough for this job.' 'If you sack me, I'll tell everyone you have a small willy,' I said. 'Yeah, that's going to work,' she replied.

I bought my wife some of that 'volume control' shampoo. Doesn't work, I can still hear her.

I don't want to think I'm getting old or anything, but all the noises I used to make during sex, I now make getting out of bed.

Just found a glove lying dead by the side of the road, the latest in a series of apparent glove suicides this winter. So sad.

A man walks by a table in a casino and passes three men and a dog playing cards. 'That's a very smart dog,' says the man. 'He's not so clever,' says one of the players. 'Every time he gets a good hand he wags his tail.'

A man walks into a bar and orders six whiskies. He lines them up in a row and knocks back the first, third and fifth glasses. Then he gets up to leave. 'Don't you want the others?' asks the bartender. 'You've only had three of your whiskies.' 'Best not,' replies the man. 'My doctor said it was only OK to have the odd drink.'

A man phones a taxi company because his cab hasn't turned up. 'I'm supposed to be at the airport for nine o'clock,' says the man. 'Don't worry,' says the girl. 'The taxi will get you there before your plane leaves.' 'I know it will,' says the man. 'I'm the pilot.'

I had a dog with no legs. I named him Cigarette so I could take him for a drag.

After twelve years of therapy my psychiatrist said something that brought tears to my eyes. He said, 'No hablo ingles.'

The only thing worse than dying alone would be dying in front of people.

You know what gets me down? An extra chromosome.

I spend far too much time wondering where the time goes.

Why do dwarfs laugh when they play football? The grass tickles their balls.

It's not you, it's me. There's only one rational human being in this relationship and it's not you, it's me.

There must be a secret slot in my dryer that makes all my socks disappear.

A gymnast walks into a bar. He gets a two-point deduction and ruins his chances of a medal.

Are my friends God's way of apologising for my relatives?

Walk a mile in my shoes and I'll seriously question your judgement. A mile's a long way: wear your own shoes and comfortable socks.

What do you call a fairy who doesn't take a bath? Stinker Bell.

You look like a Barbie!' 'Thanks, tall and beautiful right?' 'No, plastic and brainless.'

Why was the little ink blot so unhappy? Because his mother was in the pen, and they didn't know how long the sentence would be.

What did the lesbian vampire say to the other lesbian vampire? 'I'll see you next month.'

It's so sad how Lake Superior let the 'Great Lakes' tag go to its head.

If Cher could turn back time – actually turn back time – all she'd do is find a way to take back those words and make you love her. Selfish.

Who invented hugs? I mean, the first hug would have been so awkward. 'What are you doing, why are you holding me?' 'Shh, just trust me.'

All men approve of premarital sex ... until they have a daughter.

I finally gave my wife multiple orgasms, but she's still not happy. Apparently, it doesn't count if there's five years between the first and second ones.

During sex, my girlfriend always wants to talk to me. Just the other night she called me from a hotel.

'Having a dog is like having a kid.' 'Really? How much have you saved for your dog's school fees?'

I've woken up looking like somebody's worst-case scenario.

If you can make a woman laugh, you're almost there. If you're almost there and then she laughs, that's a different thing.

Stalking is when two people go for a long romantic walk together but only one of them knows it.

Just saw a red butterfly chasing a green butterfly and I didn't know butterflies did World War I re-enactments too, that's so cool.

I eat cake because it's somebody's birthday somewhere.

Why don't you slip into something more comfortable … like a coma.

I hate to brag, but I've read more than 10 per cent of the books I own.

What's 30ft long and smells like urine? Line dancing at a nursing home.

At this point, it's kind of embarrassing if your pet isn't a YouTube sensation.

Did you know drinking beer makes you smart? It made Bud wiser.

Why did the computer squeak? Someone stepped on its mouse.

The people who make medicine clearly have no idea what fruit tastes like.

The last nine hours of the working day are definitely the hardest.

'DO AS I SAY AND NOBODY GETS HURT!' would be a great way to start a health and safety demonstration.

Good morning. I see the assassins have failed.

What did the DJ order from the deli? A club sandwich with extra beets.

My doctor says he thinks I'm having a mid-life crisis. I was so surprised I nearly fell off my skateboard.

My doctor encouraged me to masturbate more often. Well, he actually told me I could have a stroke any time.

I hate it when I say something will happen 'over my dead body' and then someone kills me and does it anyway.

Is French kissing in France just called kissing?

I was having dinner with the world chess champion and there was a check tablecloth. It took him two hours to pass me the salt.

After my accident, the nurse said, 'You may not feel anything from the waist down.' 'Fair enough,' I replied, groping her breasts.

Life as a penguin can be frustrating. Even when you're seriously pissed off and waddle off in a huff, you still look cute.

I've woken up looking like a 'Don't Talk to Strangers' poster.

If you drop a white hat into the Red Sea, what does it become? Wet.

Fun fact: Most people called Kieran genuinely don't know if their name is Kieran, Keiran, Keiron or Kieren.

Neighbour 1: 'Why are you putting those jackets on your house?' Neighbour 2: 'Well, it says on the paint can to put three coats on.'

'You learn something new every day.' – Recovering amnesiac.

I tried to share a meal with a homeless guy I saw sitting on a bench last night. He told me to get lost and buy my own.

When the doctor told me I only had six months to live, I killed him violently with his own pencil. Worked a treat. Got me twenty years.

Serious question: How many times can I wear red trousers in public before people can legally murder me?

When I see a Goodfellas pizza in the freezer, I assume it's there because it betrayed the other pizzas.

The wife has just been attacked by a shark. In fairness, I probably shouldn't have taken the loan out in her name.

I'm in Melton Mowbray, telling porky pies about where I am.

We can only imagine the terrible haircuts barbers got away with before the mirror was invented.

My brother laughs at my job making the Monopoly board game. Just because he works at the Royal Mint and makes serious money.

My maths teacher staples Burger King applications on failed tests.

Football managers only say they have a selection headache to get out of joyless sex with their players.

I have a six-pack. It's under my fat. It's shy.

Reminder that if you take your dog for an hour-long walk, it's actually seven hours to them, which in bad weather could be disastrous.

What did the big chimney say to the little chimney? 'You're too young to smoke.'

I was serving some fish in my restaurant last night. One of them called me over and said, 'Excuse me, we're out of water.'

I'm no Tour de France expert but it seems that the best way to win is to wear a yellow T-shirt.

The worst part of being a cat is probably reading your own obituary eight times.

My new book, *How to Say No without Upsetting People*, has been very politely declined by publishers.

Harry gets a job painting white dotted lines down the middle of roads. On his first day he does very well and paints six miles of road. On the second day he does four miles, but on the third day he's down to only two. 'I don't understand it,' says his foreman. 'You were doing so well. What happened?' 'Well, it's obvious,' says Harry. 'Every day I'm getting further and further away from the tin of paint.'

Fun fact: Winnie the Pooh wears no pants because he was caught in bed with another bear's wife, jumped out of the window and went with it.

I was so tired this morning, I yawned and accidentally ate fifteen commuters.

It's probably time I took responsibility for my cat's hopeless addiction to Baileys Irish Cream.

'I make you laugh? I'm here to fuckin' amuse you? What do you mean "funny"? Funny how? How am I funny?' – Terrible children's entertainer.

Zombies eat brains. You're safe.

As a kid, I used to torture ants with a magnifying glass and the sun. I'd make them read it.

Which is worse, ignorance or apathy? Who knows? Who cares?

I've written a book called *How Not to Get Conned out of your Money*. It's available in all good bookshops priced £749.99.

My wife is leaving me because I spend too much time down the pub. That's the rumour down The Red Lion, anyway.

What's the opposite of Christopher Reeve? Christopher Walken.

A good girlfriend can save you about 200GB of hard disk space.

Imagine not having a favourite pair of socks.

Why did the surfer think the sea was his friend? Because it gave him a big wave.

What do you call a pig that does karate? A pork chop.

Crabs look like a chorus line sheepishly leaving the stage because they came on too soon.

I went to work with one welly on the other day. The weatherman said to expect one foot of snow.

'I just had a visit from the bailiffs' is the new 'I don't even own a TV'.

What did the laundryman say to the impatient customer? 'Keep your shirt on.'

Never bring a downhill run to an uphill battle.

Spelling … It's not exactly brian surgery is it?

How many murders is too many to admit to on a first date?

Why did the robber take a bath before he stole from the bank? He wanted to make a clean getaway.

Birthdays are good for your health. Studies have shown that people who have more birthdays live the longest.

I told the doctor I broke my leg in two places. He told me to stop going to those places.

I remember the time I smoked weed with my sister. It must have been good stuff, because I'm an only child.

I totally understand why paper and scissors don't get along. But rock? That dude's just an asshole looking for a fight.

At which Olympics did Mr T. win all his medals?

So I was driving behind this car and the kids in the back were watching cartoons and I love cartoons and ... how do I get home from Devon?

The problem with the world is the intelligent people are full of doubts while the stupid people are full of confidence.

What do a gynaecologist and a pizza boy have in common? They can smell it but they can't eat it.

Why does Wales only have stop signs at road intersections? Because Welshmen will never yield.

I fired my masseuse today. She rubbed me the wrong way.

I've woken up looking like the imaginary friend of a particularly disturbed child.

It's so sad when you think you've met the perfect girl and then you say she's 'very unique' and she beats you to death with a dictionary.

At the end of my letters, I like to write 'P. S. – this is what part of the alphabet would look like if Q and R were eliminated.'

If you tell me you're in a long-distance relationship, all I hear is 'restraining order'.

My phone will ring at two in the morning, and my wife will look at me and go, 'Who's that calling at this time?' 'I don't know! If I knew that we wouldn't need the bloody phone!'

I've just done 100 press-ups in a row … The lift attendant looked pretty annoyed.

I had a fight with an erection this morning. I beat it single-handedly.

I didn't hit you, I simply high-fived your face.

I've been holding my stomach in for about three years now so don't talk to me about dedication.

Starting to think blackbirds aren't just goths going through a phase.

An update that requires me to restart my laptop is an update that is never getting installed.

The first time I ever saw a doctor, he grabbed my leg and hit me so hard I cried, so no, I don't trust doctors.

Why do farts stink? So that deaf people can enjoy them too.

Did you know that Hannibal was the first man to experiment with genetics? He crossed a mountain with an elephant.

A screwdriver walks into a bar. The bartender says, 'Hey, we have a drink named after you!' The screwdriver responds, 'You have a drink named Murray?'

What is the difference between erotic and kinky? Erotic is using a feather … kinky is using the whole chicken.

I'm sending out spam emails about diet pills, hoping to reach a wider audience.

Why did Karl Marx dislike Earl Grey tea? Because all proper tea is theft.

I walked into the boss's office and handed him a pear. He asked, 'What's this for?' 'A pay rise. My wife told me to grow it first and then ask you.'

Million-pound-idea: Invest a billion pounds in Facebook.

Dogs have masters. Cats have staff.

Who earns a living by driving his customers away? A taxi driver.

Superstitious people must find it very hard to accept that some magpies just enjoy being single.

I'm in great mood tonight because the other day I entered a competition and I won a year's supply of Marmite. One jar.

Fun fact: Births were invented by Hallmark to sell more birthday cards.

You don't know something? Google it. You don't know someone? Facebook them. You can't find something? 'Mum!'

What do you call a lawyer with an IQ of 50? 'Your Honour.'

Ugh, am I really 1,400 lbs in dog weight?

Nothing brings two people together like the hatred of a third person.

What concert costs 45 cents? 50 Cent featuring Nickelback.

Forget beauty sleep. I want skinny sleep.
I used to be indecisive but now I'm not quite sure.

When a vegan goes missing they put them on a soya-milk carton.

The first rule of Bureaucracy Club is just the first of thousands and thousands of petty and entirely unnecessary rules.

My wife has said she is going to leave me because of my obsession with writing in to problem pages, and I don't know what to do. Sean, London.

Billie Jean is not my lover. She's my mixed doubles partner.

What monster sits on the end of your finger? The bogie man.

I'm a very generous tipper, mostly because I can't work out percentages in my head.

For sale: Anagram from my secret lout club. Buyer must collect.

'Now you've seen the best of me, come on and take the rest of me.' – Worst sales pitch ever.

Why did the Indians come to America first? Because they had reservations.

Having heard about deer antler spray, I now know how reindeer fly.

There's no sadder sight than a jet ski thinking it's time to get rid of its partner and go it alone.

Imagine how different history might be if Martin Luther King hadn't eaten so much cheese the night before his speech.

What idiot called it 'King Arthur and the knights of the round table' instead of a 'circumference sir conference'?

For many animals, the real test of anthropomorphism is learning how to pronounce the word 'anthropomorphism'.

Telling jokes about Sting's sex life takes ages, but the punch line is well worth the wait.

I love it when the baby next door cries for hours and hours, because it's nice to have something in common with young people.

Man: Am I the first man you ever made love to? Woman: You might be. Now you come to mention it, your face does look familiar.

Two men, Jack and John, go on a skiing trip and get caught in a blizzard. They pull into a farm and ask the lady of the house, a good-looking widow, if they can sleep on her sofa. She agrees, and they turn in for the night. Next morning they go on their way and enjoy a weekend of skiing. A few months later Jack gets a letter from the widow's lawyer. He says to John, 'You remember that good-looking widow we met on our skiing holiday?' 'Yes,' says John. 'Did you get up in the middle of the night, go up to her room and have sex with her?' asks Jack. 'Yes,' admits John, a little embarrassed. 'I see,' says Jack. 'And when you had sex did you happen to use my name instead of yours?' John's face turns red. 'Yeah, sorry,' he says. 'I'm afraid I did,' 'Well,' says Jack, 'you must have been damn good. She's just died and left everything to me.'

Two men are comparing notes on their summer holidays. 'I was staying in a hotel in Poole,' says one. 'In Dorset?' asks the other. 'Certainly, I'd recommend it to anyone.'

My favourite poem is 'The Waste Land'. It's a littery masterpiece.

Imagine owning a hamster and not blowing a hairdryer into his cage every morning to make him think you emigrated while he was sleeping.

Did you hear about the new 'emo' grass? People love it because it cuts itself.

Fun fact: The acoustic eel became the electric eel in 1965, causing outrage among fans.

What did the Italian say when the eel swam by? That's a Moray.

Man: How much for a hand job? Prostitute: £15. Man: Thanks. I don't want one, I just wanted to know how much I was saving every night.

Son: Mum, what's an orgasm? Wife: How would I know? Ask your dad. Me: ... Hey!

There must be gremlins in my laptop. I just spilt water all over it and now everything's going horribly wrong.

I'm told there's a book called *The Most Cynical Man in the World*, but I'm not buying it.

Boy, those people older than us and younger than us sure are stupid, right?

If we aren't supposed to eat animals, then why are they made out of meat?

Got an email that said 'Want to see Justin Bieber live?' At first I thought it was a ransom demand.

I'm trying to write a joke about unemployed people. But it needs more work.

The new Doctor Who is Glaswegian. The first episode will see him in his hometown, fighting hordes of Cidermen.

I'm hoping that what I lack in self-awareness, I more than make up for in something brilliant that I'm just not aware of yet.

Two turtles bump into each other. 'Slow down,' the first turtle says. The second replies, 'Touch me again and there'll be shell to pay.'

Sadly, Mr Nice Guy comes from a long line of Dr Nice Guys and is a huge disappointment to his family.

Warning: Dates in calendar are closer than they appear.

What kind of flowers have lips? Tulips.

Does the name Pavlov ring a bell?

How do you make a plumber cry? You kill his family.

A couple on my train are talking so loudly I think they're accidentally pressing 'Reply to all' before they speak.

When the going gets tough, I cry like a baby and wonder if I'm cut out for this cruel world.

Action speaks louder than words but not nearly as often.

People who demand 'Bullet points, not *War and Peace*!' have no idea how useful an insight into Tsarist society in the Napoleonic era can be.

I think my eyesight's fine, but this judge disagrees. He says I need supervision.

Why does Miss Piggy douche with honey? Because Kermit likes sweet and sour pork.

I drove my car into a river and watched it turn into a mobile phone. One minute, a Kia. Next minute, Nokia.

When meeting your girlfriend's mum for the first time always push her over to see what your girlfriend's balance will be like when she's older.

They held hands, kissed tenderly and walked off into the sunset. Sadly, they burnt horribly on arrival.

'Mum,' asked the small girl, 'do you mind if my exam results are like a submarine?' 'What do you mean?' asked the mother. 'Below C level.'

Why did the tiny ghost join the football squad? He heard they needed a little team spirit.

The only time a fisherman tells the truth is when he calls another fisherman a liar.

Unless you can be Batman, always be yourself.

I bought a box of animal crackers and it said on it, 'Do not eat if seal is broken.' So I opened up the box, and sure enough…

'My children are also my best friends.' – Lonely parent.

My 'check engine' light came on while driving to work this morning. I looked and the engine is still there.

I just did a speed reading course. Read *War and Peace*. It was about Russia.

Just changed all my passwords to 'incorrect'. So my computer reminds me 'incorrect password' when I forget.

My wife and I were married in a toilet – it was a marriage of convenience.

You call it armed robbery; I call it people giving me gifts to celebrate my new gun.

What's black, white and red all over? A skunk with nappy rash.

Why did the British think that the Boston Tea Party was barbaric? No one added milk.

I was told never go to bed on an argument and to cut a long story short I haven't been to bed since 2007.

I went down the local supermarket and I said, 'I want to make a complaint, this vinegar's got lumps in it.' He said, 'Those are pickled onions.'

I love that my nephew's book, *The Importance of Sharing*, has a 'This Book Belongs To…' bit at the front.

I've woken up looking like a vaguely amusing story on page 9 of the local paper.

Want to hear a joke about sodium? Na.

A Haiku about getting out of bed: No No No No No No No No No No No No No No No No No.

I got pulled over for drunk driving. But honestly, in my defence, I didn't even know I was driving.

Why doesn't Spiderman like rice? It reminds him of Uncle Ben.

My wife plays the piano by ear. Sometimes her earrings get in the way.

There's no sadder sight than a tortoise storming off in a huff.

If you're honest, generous, funny and kind, I will love you unconditionally.

What did the one penny say to the other penny? We make perfect cents.

To whoever stole my copy of Microsoft Office: I will find you. You have my Word.

My wife is *really* angry with me. Because I didn't know why she was angry with me in the first place.

Why did the orange use suntan lotion? He started to peel.

If one is single and two is a couple and three is a crowd, what is four and five? Nine.

Why did the book get stitches? Because he had his appendix removed.

Whenever I delete an app from my iPhone, the shaking icons make me think they're panicked over who's being cut from the team.

If you want to find out who's been avoiding tax, just go to Google and ... it's them.

I just ate something which disagreed with me and now I have a bone to pick.

I've got a friend who has a butler whose left arm is missing. Serves him right.

I'm going to start treating people the way I want to be treated, so I'm going to start taking off my shirt in front of every girl I meet.

Is a hippopotamus a hippopotamus? Or just a really cool opotamus?

One in ten people have tried LSD. Probably because it was easier to get than Sudafed.

An elderly woman returns home and finds her husband in bed with a young woman. Enraged, she flings him out of the window and watches him plummet to his death.

At her trial she pleads not guilty to murder. 'How can you plead not guilty?' asks the prosecuting lawyer. 'You threw your husband to his death.' 'I didn't know he was going to die,' replies the woman. 'I reckoned if he could still commit adultery aged ninety-eight there was a good chance he could fly, too.'

A hangover is the wrath of grapes.

Many years ago I had washboard abs but now I have a front loader.

Hot shingles in your area!

Convince your boss you're full of ambition by spending entire meetings practising your autograph.

Tell a therapist, not Facebook.

No one ever went to the grave saying, 'I wish I had eaten more rice cakes.'

I've woken up looking like a terrible secret that's about to tear a family apart.

What's the definition of a will? ... Come on, guys. The answer's a dead giveaway.

When I see one of my pals online late at night, I like to give them a scare and text them, 'MATE, turn off your bloody webcam.'

I visited the offices of the RSPCA today. Blimey, it was tiny. You couldn't swing a cat in there.

I found out today that using spit as lube is not cool. And it's also enough to get you sacked as a prostate examiner.

What do a baker and a millionaire have in common? They're both rolling in the dough.

Cocktail umbrellas: If the glass beneath you is full, you're a terrible umbrella.

Yoghurts are the suicide bombers of packed lunches.

A marketing tool is a good way to describe anyone who works in marketing.

What do cannibals eat for elevenses? A football team.

My doctor said, 'You've got a very serious illness.' I said, 'I want a second opinion.' He said, 'All right, you're ugly as well.'

Rule no. 1 for arguments: If you're losing, start correcting their grammar.

A bee flying around your office is a lot more fun if you pretend it's a traffic warden in an out-of-control hot-air balloon.

Me + mathematics = syntax error

Wouldn't it be nice if retail therapy was covered by health insurance?

Why does the hipster make crappy coffee? The beans are always under-ground.

I always sleep with a knife under my pillow, just in case. (Just in case I want to eat cheese in the middle of the night.)

I went for a run but came back after two minutes because I forgot something. I forgot I'm out of shape and can't run for more than two minutes.

Whenever I see my wife's tampon string I can't help but wonder if she's just an angry puppet who cut herself free.

Over the internet, you can pretend to be anyone or anything. I'm amazed that so many people choose to be complete twats.

How do you make a fire with two sticks? Make sure one is a match.

The world is £4 trillion in debt. Just exactly which planet do we owe it to?

What do a near-sighted gynaecologist and a puppy have in common? A wet nose.

What has two thumbs and couldn't care less? A ransom demand.

Every time I think I've hit the bottom, someone lends me a shovel.

My new book is called *Wooooaaooooh*. I now regret using a ghost writer.

What did one toilet say to the other? 'You look a bit flushed.'

I don't remember being absent-minded.

I'll start to believe that video games create violent killings the day someone gets arrested for killing a pig by catapulting a bird at it.

After being a heavy smoker for the last thirty years I found myself severely out of breath whenever I ran to catch a bus, so I've given up. I'll just walk, and wait for the next one in future.

My wife is really into DIY. Every time I ask her to fix something, she says, 'Oh, do it yourself!'

Spend all day every day loading up on carbohydrates in case you ever decide to run a marathon.

Why did the hedgehog cross the road? To see his flat mate.

When the nurse told my mother she had an eight-pound bundle of joy, she said, 'Thank God, the laundry's back!'

If you get angry, just relax, take a deep breath and count to ten. Unless of course you're angry about oxygen and numbers.

I still think Barack Obama stole 'Yes We Can' from Bob the Builder.

My nan once told me that when she was younger she had to beat men off with a stick. Sex must have been pretty weird back then.

Of course we can be friends! Just not with each other.

Every story worth repeating ends with the admonition 'let's never speak of this again'.

I learned how to beat people up on an assault course.

Ever since my wife left me for being an alcoholic, I can't stop drinking about her.

I can keep secrets, it's the people I tell who can't.

What kind of jam can't you eat? A traffic jam.

People found guilty of not using punctuation deserve the longest sentence possible.

In a school of fish, red herrings are notorious for distracting their classmates.

A man goes to the doctor's. The doctor says, 'Go to the window. Stick your tongue out.' The man asks, 'Why?' The doctor says, 'I don't like my neighbours.'

What did the pencil say to the paper? 'I dot my i's on you.'

Russian dolls are so full of themselves.

'You are what you eat.' That's funny, I don't remember eating a legend lately.

What's a pirate's favourite treat? Chips AHOY!

So sad how the volleyball in *Cast Away* was let down by Hollywood and never acted again.

Time flies when you're throwing watches.

'This is all your fault!' my wife moaned. 'What have I done now?' I asked her. 'Give me a chance to think,' she said, 'I only just woke up.'

What should you do if your girlfriend starts smoking? Slow down. And possibly use a lubricant.

There's no I in anxiety. Wait. Yes there is. Oh my god oh my god oh my god.

A student travelling on a train looks up and sees Einstein sitting next to him. Excited, he asks, 'Excuse me, Professor. Does Boston stop at this train?'

They say women are attracted to men who treat them badly. So when a gorgeous lady came to me with a swollen ankle, I gave her cough medicine.

I've just got an off-the-books job as a gynaecologist. It's all gash in hand.

My niece once had a boyfriend with a wooden leg, but she broke it off.

The tangled mess I just made of my headphones reminds me I'd be a terrible spider.

Nice one Captain Obvious. You're welcome, Sergeant Sarcasm! Indeed, Comrade Comeback. Thank you, Senior Smartass. Any time, Dictator Dickhead.

'Why the hell did you call me a control freak?' I asked my wife, angrily. 'Because you told me to!' she cried.

Despite Gloria Estefan's promises, the rhythm never did get me.

It's so sad that Jesus never really made the most of his carpentry qualifications.

I wasn't great at maths in school, so the three words I feared the most were 'pop quiz.'

My train has been stuck outside the station so long, I've started to compile a list of which passengers I'll eat first if it comes to that.

Two sausages are sizzling in a pan. One sausage turns to the other and says, 'It's hot in here!' The other sausage replies, 'Hey, a talking sausage!'

The kids text me 'plz' because it's shorter than 'please'. I text back 'no' because it's shorter than 'yes'.

One of the toddlers on the intensive care unit is playing with a toy donkey. ICU baby, shaking that ass.

Wine improves with age. I improve with wine.

Why did the chicken commit suicide? To get to the other side.

What do you call a story about a broken pencil? Pointless.

Einstein said 'imagination is more important than knowledge'. But if you have knowledge of the right websites you don't need your imagination.

Why did the calendar write its will? Its days were numbered.

I need a good night's sleep tonight. I have to be at work tomorrow and also the forty years after tomorrow.

When I argue with my wife, I always get the last word. It's just that sometimes she can't hear it.

I knew you were drunk last night when you cooked pizza for 200 minutes at 18 degrees.

Got chatted up by a large lady in the pub, 'So, what do you do?' Responding with, 'Not fat chicks!' was totally worth the drink in the face.

Every day, you should do something that scares you. I look at Facebook.

What do you call a dog that loves dance music? Subwoofer.

I'd hate to be a giraffe with a sore throat.

It's all fun and games until you check your bank statement in the morning.

Were you long in the hospital? No, I was the same size I am now.

Got slapped by a girl for asking 'Do you spit or swallow?' I thought this was a reasonable question since we were at a wine tasting session.

If you don't stop giving me ultimatums, we're finished.

'Don't tell me what happened, I'm recording it.' – Terrible undercover agent.

It's my first day working in the library. So, to make a good impression, I've organised all the books by size.

What's black, white and red all over and doesn't fit through a revolving door? A nun with a spear through her head.

I bet the main reason the police keep people away from a plane crash is they don't want anybody walking in and lying down in the crash stuff, and then, when somebody comes up, acting like they just woke up and going, 'What was that?!'

Today I woke up and realised my muffin top has become a pound cake.

Convince people you're a spy by parking your car over the road from their house and taking photos of them as they leave.

A drunk was brought into a police station. He pounded his fist on the counter and said, 'I want to know why I've been arrested.' The sergeant said, 'You have been brought in for drinking.' He said, 'Oh, that's all right, then. Let's get started!'

America is the country where everyone has the right to remain silent but no one has the ability.

The pen is writier than the sword.

Tough day. Just had to tell my screenplay he's adapted.

Current relationship status: Going on walking holiday with grandparents.

Just found a half-finished crossword on the train. Now need CCTV to find whoever's responsible so I can show them where they went wrong.

A Pakistani, a homosexual, and a Jew walk into a bar. What a fine example of an integrated community.

What's the difference between Jesus and a picture of Jesus? It only takes one nail to hang a picture of Jesus.

How are doughnuts and golf alike? They both have a hole in one.

'We are standing on the shoulders of giants.' – Parrots.

I went to the paper shop. It had blown away.

I'm recovering from a cold. I'm so full of penicillin that if I sneeze I'll cure someone.

Don't break anyone's heart; they only have one. Break their bones; they have over 206 of them.

Did you hear about the testicular cancer survivor who won the lottery? When he found out, the guy went nut.

To this day, the boy who used to bully me at school still takes my lunch money. On the plus side, he makes great sandwiches.

My brain is giving me the silent treatment today.

Idea for a TV show: A mixed grill uses DNA technology to research its family tree. Laughs, tears and one or two surprises ensue.

A Get Well Soon card is a nice way to add undue pressure to a work colleague's recovery from illness.

I was watching Jurassic park the other day, when I thought, 'Not only does my son have a stupid name, but he's also a shit driver.'

It's so sad that paper aeroplanes are too flammable to meet modern aviation safety standards.

Why should you never tell a secret in a corn field? Because there are too many ears.

My brain is like a clown car for bad ideas.

In most cases, TV detectives need at least seven people to be murdered before they find the killer, and yet they get series after series. Crazy.

Note to self: Stop sending yourself silly notes.

If you can't laugh at yourself, who can you laugh at? I start with other people, then penguins, then back to other people.

Breaking news: A mass fight has broken out in a petrol station. Twenty-three people arrested in Total.

I phoned up Drugs Awareness today. I said, 'Can I speak to a cocaine councillor please?' He said, 'You'll have to wait, he's on another line.'

If water tasted more like wine, I would have no problem drinking eight glasses a day.

We feed our baby onions so we can find him in the dark at night.

Two interesting facts about me: 1. My knob is the same length as two Argos pens. 2. I'm banned from Argos.

What do cow pies and cowgirls have in common? The older they get the easier they are to pick up.

A man is walking down the street, when a mugger pulls out a knife and says, 'Your money or your life!' An extremely long silence follows. 'Your money or your life!' the thug repeats. Finally, the man says, 'I'm thinking!'

What do people in China call their good-quality plates?

What kind of underwear do reporters wear? News briefs.

How come ignorance is bliss, but it's the not knowing that really hurts? You can't have it both ways!

What do you call two crows on a branch? Attempted murder.

What did the little boy's mum say when he asked her to buy him shoes for gym? 'Tell Jim to buy his own shoes.'

So I went to a Chinese restaurant and this duck came up to me with a red rose and says, 'Your eyes sparkle like diamonds.' I said, 'Waiter, I asked for a-ROMATIC duck.'

When I tell women I served in Iraq it's easy to get laid. No point adding I got knocked out in the qualifying round of the Baghdad Tennis Open.

Got a new job at the old folks' home as a comedian. Bless 'em, they don't get the jokes … but they still piss themselves.

'There's a special place in Hell for people like you!' – The Hell Tourist Board.

After my prostate exam, the doctor left. Then the nurse came in. As she shut the door, she whispered the three words no man wants to hear: 'Who was that?'

Biggest lie ever: I accept these terms and conditions.

LA is so celebrity-conscious, there's a restaurant that only serves Jack Nicholson – and when he shows up, they tell him there'll be a ten-minute wait.

There are three kinds of people in this world. Those who can count and those who can't.

I'm allergic to food. Every time I eat I break out into fat.

It's great when the person next to me on a train tells me all about their day, as my brain completely switches off and relaxes for an hour.

You do not have to say anything, but it may harm your defence if you do not mention when questioned how very nice my new haircut looks.

I think car horns should sound like gun shots ... I bet you'll move then.

How do you stop a dog from humping your leg? Pick him up and suck on his cock.

If practice makes perfect and no one's perfect, what's the point of practice?

I said to my doctor, 'With the excitement of Christmas, I can't sleep.' He said, 'Try lying on the edge of the bed, you'll soon drop off.'

People who think living well is the best revenge have clearly never broken into someone's house and sewn all their clothes together.

What do you call a poor Italian neighbourhood? A spaghetto.

The first rule of Exaggeration Club is: do not talk about Exaggeration Club – but there are millions of other rules to remember too.

If people could read my mind, I'd probably owe them a cigarette.

What did Sushi A say to Sushi B? WASSA-B!

I wish conversations were like user agreements where I could skip to the end and just agree.

A terrible attitude problem means never having to say you're sorry.

Vegas is an amazing place. I went to visit in a $30,000 car and left in a $200,000 bus.

Why are pubic hairs so curly? So they don't poke her eye out.

Did you hear about the Native American who drank 1,000 glasses of tea? He drowned in his tea pee.

Where should a 500-pound alien go? On a diet.

A man walks into a fishmonger's carrying a salmon under his arm. 'Do you make fishcakes?' he asks. 'Of course,' says the fishmonger. 'Oh good,' says the man. 'It's his birthday.'

A writer dies and St Peter offers him the choice of heaven or hell. To see what he has in store St Peter takes him to hell, where rows of writers are chained to their desks and are being whipped by demons in a steaming dungeon. However, when they get to heaven the writer is astonished to see that nothing has changed: rows of writers are chained to their desks and are being whipped by demons in a steaming dungeon. 'Hey!' says the writer. 'This is just as bad as hell.' 'No, it's not,' replies St Peter. 'Up here you get published.'

When does a cub become a boy scout? When he eats his first brownie.

She asked for a mixed tape so I gave her pâté but she said there are no diacritics in tape and this is how all great romances start, right?

Early mornings are great for spending time with the family. Then they spoil it by waking up.

I'm a pint of milk short of the full delivery. Call the men in white coats!

American stereotypes are like British stereotypes, but with much nicer teeth.

Did you hear about the cannibal who committed suicide? He got himself into a real stew.

There are 10 types of people in this world. Those that know binary, and those that don't.

Women forgive and forget but they always make sure you don't forget that they forgave you and forgot about it.

An optimist is someone who falls off the Empire State Building, and after fifty floors says, 'So far so good!'

As a woman, my wife doesn't always know exactly what she wants but she knows she's going to be mad as hell if she doesn't get it.

Just won a fantastic prize in a Doctor Who competition. Two tickets for the 1966 World Cup Final.

What did Batman say to Robin before they got in the car? Get in the car.

What kind of phones do people in jail use? Cell phones.

Just noticed exclamation marks look like thin people exploding out of their shoes!

My girlfriend just bought a ruler from Smiths. Heaven knows I'm measurable now.

How do hair stylists speed up their job? They take short cuts.

My house isn't messy. It's custom-designed by a three-year-old.

Fool around with an admirer if you want to get married.

Job interview: 'What would you say was your greatest weakness?' 'Honesty.' 'I don't think honesty is a weakness.' 'I don't give a fuck what you think.'

'I don't normally do this on a first date' is a fun thing to say while wearing a clown costume and singing the Danish national anthem.

I called my lawyer and said, 'Can I ask you two questions?' He said, 'What's the second question?'

I hate those unrealistic films where people do interesting things and become better people.

So I rang up a local building firm and I said, 'I want a skip outside my house.' He said, 'I'm not stopping you.'

How much of this 'no more tears' shampoo do I have to feed this baby to get it to stop crying?

I saw a man take a gate from the bottom of my garden. I didn't say anything; I didn't want him to take a fence.

Make power cuts more emotional by telling your torch that this is its moment to shine.

Why did the sea monster eat five ships that were carrying potatoes? No one can eat just one potato ship.

Sky News would be a great name for a weather channel.

Calling yourself a lifelong fan is a nice way of admitting you've never grown out of your childhood obsessions.

Why did the dinosaur walk across the road? Because chickens hadn't been invented yet.

Not everyone sleeping in doorways is genuinely homeless. Many are private detectives who were paid to spy on boring people and fell asleep.

'Well, Jean-Paul Sartre's nothing special either.' – Other People.

Fun fact: The word brunch originated in the 1960s, when busy executives would break mid-morning to eat broccoli and Monster Munch.

An old farmer and his wife were leaning against the edge of their pigsty when the old woman wistfully recalled that the next week would mark their golden wedding anniversary. 'Let's have a party,' she suggested. 'Let's kill a pig.' The farmer scratched his grizzled head. 'Well, Ethel,' he finally answered, 'I don't see why the pig should take the blame for something that happened fifty years ago.'

I think you'll find that any of my lady companions will tell you I'm a 'five-times-a-night-man'. I really shouldn't drink so much tea before I go to bed.

Blonde girl: What does idk stand for? Me: I don't know. Blonde: Oh my God, nobody does!

How do you kill a circus clown? Go for the juggler!

Boy: Want to hear a joke about my dick? Never mind, it's too long. Girl: Wanna hear a joke about my pussy? Never mind, you won't get it.

Why was the football team hot? It didn't have any fans.

Getting a job repairing revolving doors was a real turning point in my life.

I've woken up looking like an *X-Factor* contestant who just found out his family were lying when they said he could sing.

Shoplifting drives up the price of merchandise for the consumers. I've found a way around that though: I buy my products from shoplifters.

Optimists/pessimists with OCD are furious when their glass is 51 per cent full/empty.

Always check with HR before sacrificing a goat in the office.

I am so excited about the insomnia convention in two weeks' time. Only zero sleeps to go.

Have I told you lately that I love you? Last night? Did I really? Fifty times? I need to stop drinking.

Brain freeze: Legitimate issue or zombie treat?

No, I don't want to come to your cat's birthday party, you freak … My dog's getting married that weekend.

My girlfriend left me because I've put on weight. She even said that my thumbs were too fat. Botch.

An unkindness of ravens must look at a murder of crows and think 'those guys take things way too far!'

I bought a book on obedience seven years ago, but it turns out the dog is a slow reader.

A bartender is just a pharmacist with a limited inventory.

'I always see the best in people.' – Failed caricaturist.

Don't tell me a tomato is 'technically a fruit' unless you're willing to drink it in a milkshake.

People keep saying prison is no holiday camp, but the bunk beds and singsongs suggest otherwise.

I asked my friend, 'How do you abbreviate Arkansas?' He said, 'I don't know, just start spelling it, and then quit.'

There are no limits to what you can accomplish when you're supposed to be doing something else.

Really nervous. Just off to meet my new girlfriend's expectations for the first time.

What can you hold without using your hands? Your breath.

Where do all the letters sleep? In the alphabed.

My sister just had a baby boy and she's asked me to be the godfather. So I've made her an offer she can't refuse.

Why do women rub their eyes when they get up in the morning? They don't have balls to scratch.

What do you call the king of vegetables? Elvis Parsley.

With age comes experience. Also, grey hair, aching bones and memory loss. Still, good news about the experience.

One day I'll look up from my phone and realise my kids put me in a nursing home.

Just gave two slices of bread a two-minute makeover in the toaster and they've popped back up looking HOT!

An over-the-shoulder stare followed by a seductive lick of the lips is one of the sexiest things in the world. Not during a rectal exam, though.

On a flight I asked the stewardess, 'Can you telephone from this plane?' She said, 'Of course I can … A plane's a big thing with wings.'

Three men were walking through the forest when they came upon a set of tracks. The first said, 'Those are deer tracks.' The second said, 'No, those are elk tracks.' The third said, 'You're both wrong, those are moose tracks.' They were still arguing when the train hit them.

The psychology instructor had just finished a lecture on mental health and was giving an oral test. Speaking specifically about manic depression, she asked, 'How would you diagnose a patient who walks back and forth screaming at the top of his lungs one minute, then sits in a chair weeping uncontrollably the next?' A young man at the back raised his hand and answered, 'A football manager?'

It's so sad that hundreds of my phone calls have been recorded, but not one has been used for training and quality purposes.

Curiouser & Curiouser would be a good name for a husband and wife team of private detectives.

Where did the music teacher leave his keys? In the piano.

I put fruit on top of my waffles, because I want something to brush off.

I was getting into my car and this bloke says to me, 'Can you give me a lift?' I said, 'Sure, you look great, the world's your oyster, go for it.'

The universe implodes. No matter.

What did Cinderella say when her photos did not show up? 'Someday my prints will come.'

It's so wrong how shoe shops keep the left shoe apart from the right shoe and guilt-trip you into reuniting them.

How many surrealists does it take to screw in a light bulb? A fish.

I can usually judge how attractive a woman is by how many times my wife calls her a whore.

A-Ha: If the sun always shone on my TV, I'd simply draw the curtains. No need to make a song and dance about it.

My new book, *Punctuality for 2012*, comes out next week.

Bull sharks are breeding in freshwater rivers and lakes, in case you ran out of things to worry about.

I got home from work and the wife said, 'I'm very sorry dear, but the cat's eaten your dinner.' I said, 'Don't worry – I'll get you a new cat.'

A policeman knocked on my door and said 'Your dog's been chasing someone on a bike.' I said, 'Don't be stupid, my dog's not got a bike.'

I used to work in a shoe recycling shop. It was sole destroying.

Bonfire Night is an annual reminder of how useless my dog would be in a war.

What gets wetter the more it dries? A towel.

A man has three knees. A right knee, a left knee and a weenie.

Most accidents occur in the home. Many men use this as an excuse to stay out late.

I don't understand why people sob quietly. Use a megaphone for crying out loud!

If there's something weird and it don't look good. Who ya gonna call? Probably a doctor.

When I wake up I make plans / To go out and achieve / Great things but then my bed hugs me / And begs me not to leave.

After twenty years of marriage, I still get blow jobs. If my wife finds out, she'll kill me.

I went to see *Les Misérables*. I came out More Misérables.

After a holiday, the only thing that makes me happy to see the people I work with is having just been with the people I'm related to.

Why was the blonde upset when she got her driver's licence? Because she got an F in sex.

I think animal testing is a terrible idea: they get all nervous and give the wrong answers.

Fun fact: If you drown in the South Pacific, a musical version of your life flashes before your eyes.

What do you get when you cross a duck with cheese? Cheese and quackers.

A neutron walks into a bar. 'I'd like a beer,' he says. The bartender promptly serves up a beer. 'How much will that be?' asks the neutron. 'For you?' replies the bartender. 'No charge.'

If you want to improve your golf, go on a course.

I saw this wino lying in a gutter eating grapes, I was like, 'bro, you have to wait'.

I went to the butchers. I bet him fifty quid that he couldn't reach the meat off the top shelf. He said, 'The steaks are too high.'

Sometimes I wrap myself in bows and call myself gifted.

Where do hippos go to school? The Hippocampus.

Vampires? They're a pain in the neck.

'North Korea plans nuclear test targeting US.' At first I was alarmed at reading this, then I realised they meant the United States.

Last year I deducted 10,697 cartons of cigarettes as a business expense. The tax man said, 'Don't ever let us catch you without a cigarette in your hand.'

Why did the girl sit on the ladder to sing? She wanted to reach the high notes.

Did you hear about the Mexican racist? He joined the que que que.

Police Chief: As a recruit, you'll be faced with some difficult issues. What would you do if you had to arrest your mother? New recruit: Call for backup!

Nurse: Doctor, the man you just gave a clean bill of health to dropped dead as he was leaving the surgery. Doctor: Turn him around. Make it look as if he was just walking in.

My darling, I've been so desolate ever since I broke off our engagement; devastated! Won't you please consider coming back to me? You hold a place in my heart no other woman can fill. I can never find another woman like you. I need you so much. Won't you forgive me and let us make a new beginning? I love you so. Yours always and truly, John. P.S. Congratulations on your lottery win.

A man goes into a barber's shop advertising David Beckham-style cuts. Half an hour later he's horrified to see his head half bald and covered in cuts. 'That's not how David Beckham has his hair,' complains the man. 'It would be if he came in here,' replies the barber.

I wouldn't say my wife lies about her age – but does she really expect people to believe that she gave birth to our son at the age of three?

Sadly, you *can* hurry love, whether you mean to or not.

I'm just a boy, standing in front of a girl, asking her to find clumsy film references witty and engaging.

I used the self-checkout at Tesco and was made employee of the month.

Dildos are illegal in Texas but guns aren't. Probably explains the low number of dildo-related murders in the area.

I've just seen a placard that read 'God hates fags'. I thought, 'At £7 a pack, I'm not surprised.'

My girlfriend and I split up because we were in different places in our relationship. I was at her sister's.

'Scientists reveal there are fewer than 100 adult cod in the whole North Sea.' Clearly, the cod population has taken a battering.

Me: Dad, how does it feel having an awesome son? Dad: I don't know, ask your grandad.

It's so sad that birthday cakes don't live long enough to have birthdays of their own.

Two old ladies are in a restaurant. One complains, 'You know, the food here is just terrible.' The other shakes her head and adds, 'And such small portions.'

A redhead tells her blonde stepsister, 'I slept with a Brazilian…' The blonde replies, 'Oh my God! You slut! How many is a brazilian?'

Sitting on Brighton beach with legs so white they're listening to Dido at a dinner party.

What part of the turkey is musical? The drumstick.

I asked the waiter, 'How do you prepare your chickens?' 'Nothing special, sir. We just tell them straight out that they're going to die.'

Convince loved ones the afterlife exists by secretly writing your autobiography and giving it to a psychic the week before you die.

Just played Cluedo: the Tudor edition. Henry VII did it, with a shovel, in the car park.

I knocked on my neighbour's door at 3 a.m. and said, 'Look, mate, some of us have to work tomorrow.' I love taking the piss out of the unemployed.

My missus says I'm having a mid-life crisis. I nearly fell off my pogo stick.

What did one tooth say to the other tooth? 'The dentist is taking me out tonight.'

Got up at 6 a.m. today. Did yoga. Had a protein shake. Ran six miles. Started lying about everything.

What do you call a pig in an aeroplane? A pig.

A burrito is a sleeping bag for ground beef.

Cop: Why were you speeding? Me: I'm going to the store to get Oreos. Cop: Double stuffed? Me: Of course. Cop: Carry on.

'I agree with you 100 per cent' is probably my favourite way of saying 'I got distracted and have absolutely no idea what you just said'.

Back in my day a flash mob was a bunch of perverts in trench coats.

6 out of 9 people will see something dirty in this sentence.

It's so sad that after silent movies went out of fashion, silent people gradually became extinct.

Imagine looking in the mirror and not bursting into tears.

What's the name of the archaeologist who works at Scotland Yard? Sherlock Bones.

If I said I love quoting Perry Como songs, would you say a) You're adorable b) You're so beautiful or c) You're a cutie full of charms?

Chickens don't have friends. They only have pen pals.

I knocked on Bruce Banner's door and told him all about global warming. He was so angry he said he was going to turn green immediately.

Why is Santa so jolly? Because he knows where all the naughty girls live.

Just found out the speaking clock isn't really a clock that can speak, and now everything's ruined.

I can neither confirm nor deny these allegations of evasiveness.

I forgot to drink responsibly again. Always read the small print.

I have no problem with you speaking your mind … as long as you can do it with your mouth closed.

I bought some new London Bridge brand jeans. They keep falling down.

No amount of medical research will find a cure as effective as when your mum kisses the place that hurts.

I stopped a guy in the street and said, 'Can you help me? I'm looking for a rubbish tip.' He said, 'Arsenal to win the Premiership.'

I don't want everything. Most of it has to be fed, fixed or dusted.

Tortoises look like soldiers sulking because their helmet was too big and slipped off.

Poker's like a séance: you sit around a table holding hands, and one guy profits from everyone else's loss.

Is it solipsistic in here, or is it just me?

Just smoking an electronic cigarette after some electronic sex.

I just got back from my best friend's funeral. He died after being hit on the head with a tennis ball. It was a lovely service.

A man walked into the doctor's. The doctor said, 'I haven't seen you in a long time.' The man replied, 'I know I've been ill.'

I don't think I could ever stab someone. I mean, let's be honest. I can barely get the straw through the Capri Sun.

Why did the Mexican girl get pregnant? Her teacher told her to go home and do an essay.

Sadly, most spiders are actually octopuses that couldn't find the ocean and became more and more emaciated.

Never run away from your problems, unless your problems are overweight security guards who just caught you shoplifting.

1. Mark spot on map. 2. Add note saying 'If anything happens, the money's buried here'. 3. Put map in suit pocket. 4. Give suit to charity shop.

Three-quarter length trousers ... for people who look a twat in shorts, but have a tattoo they want you to see.

Oral sex. A taste of things to come.

Marriage counselling. Because sometimes your wife needs to hear from a professional that she's being a bitch.

Whenever my mate Dave starts stuttering, I always try and lighten the mood. By pretending to scratch invisible turntables.

What's the difference between a fish and a piano? You can tune a piano, but you can't tuna fish.

My petrol tank just went from zero to £50 in under a minute.

Just so you know, Sleeping Beauty was probably a one-off. I just tried kissing a sleeping woman on a bus and that didn't end happily at all.

I blame that ticket inspector who was rude to me in 2011 for all my misplaced anger issues.

How do you know if your boyfriend has a high sperm count? You have to chew before you swallow.

I was the class clown at school. Well, I was the only boy wearing make-up, anyway.

Why do you go to bed every night? Because the bed won't come to you.

If someone says I look like a spy, does that mean I do look like a spy or I don't look like a spy?

What's the hardest part of rollerblading? Telling your parents that you're gay.

I want my children to be independent, headstrong people. Just not while I'm raising them.

It's not my place to tell others how to do their job, but carrying a swag bag and calling yourself the Hamburglar is just asking to get caught.

Even on Valentine's Day, my secret admirers take the secret part seriously. Good for them.

What do you get when you have fifty female pigs and fifty male deer? One hundred sows and bucks.

What do envelopes say when you lick them? Nothing, it shuts them up.

How many programmers does it take to change a light bulb? None, it's a hardware problem.

Whenever I delete text messages, I feel like I'm deleting evidence.

Did you hear about the Mexican train killer? He had loco motives.

Wearing a deep sea diver's watch is just asking to be eaten by punctual, fashion-conscious sharks.

I don't have a microwave oven, but I do have a clock that occasionally cooks stuff.

Sometimes, it's almost like asking for the waitress to be dressed in a bear costume is taking ordering off-menu too far.

In order to get a loan, you first need to prove that you don't need it.

What kind of dress can't be worn? Address.

I've woken up looking like the self-portrait of a particularly distressed child.

You're only your own worst critic until we become friends.

An old man goes to a school reunion where he finds that his surviving classmates are only interested in talking about their ailments: kidney stones, heart murmurs, liver pains etc. When he gets home his daughter asks him how it went. 'It wasn't much of a reunion,' he replies. 'It was more like an organ recital.'

A man is in a bar talking to his friend. 'Last night, while I was out drinking, a burglar broke into my house.' 'Did he get anything?' asks his friend. 'Yes,' says the man. 'A broken jaw, six teeth knocked out and a pair of broken ribs. My wife thought it was me coming home drunk.'

What do you call a Frenchman in sandals? Philippe Philoppe.

I'm sick of following my dreams. I'm going to ask them where they're going and hook up with them later.

The more you learn about people who claim to have been abducted by aliens, the more you understand why the aliens let them come home.

What does it mean when your boyfriend is in your bed gasping for breath and calling your name? You didn't hold the pillow down long enough.

I need a six-month holiday, twice a year.

I really should stop ending relationships just because we can't agree which Mr Man I'm most like.

I never look down on any woman. Unless they are showing some awesome cleavage.

What did Mr T say when he saw a fat lady at the bar? I pity the stool!

Boss: I don't get down to your office much. Me: And don't think we don't appreciate that.

Sad to hear the schools are breaking up just months after they got back together.

Taking shoelaces away from depressed people is stupid because wearing shoes without laces will look silly and make them even more depressed.

An old gentleman goes to his doctor to complain about a problem with his sex drive. 'I don't seem to have as much pep as I used to,' he tells the doctor. 'I see,' says the doctor. 'And how old are you and your wife?' 'I'm eighty-two,' says the man, 'and my wife is seventy-eight.' 'And when did you first notice the problem?' asks the doctor. The old man replies, 'Twice last night and once again this morning.'

A man goes into a bookshop and asks the assistant, 'Do you keep stationery?' 'No,' she replies. 'Sometimes I wriggle about a bit.'

A ship's captain radios a lighthouse keeper. 'Radio reception is very bad. Please spell out your weather report.' The keeper replies, 'W-E-T-H-O-R-R-E-P-O-R-T.' 'My God,' says the captain, 'that's the worst spell of weather I've had in a long time.'

I was stealing things in the shop balanced on the shoulders of a couple of vampires. I was charged with shoplifting on two counts.

My wife told me she's loving me because I don't listen to her properly.

When one door closes, another door opens. I need a new car.

I didn't want to get into bed last night. Now I have Stockholm Syndrome.

Lazy stereotypes are best avoided on St Patrick's Day. At least until lunchtime, after which the Irish will be far too drunk to notice.

The journey of a thousand miles begins with a broken fan belt and a flat tyre.

I miss your absence.

Where do giant spiders play football? At Webley Stadium.

People who cry when chopping onions but then roast baby carrots and feel nothing are the worst hypocrites on earth.

A horse walked into a bar. Several people got up and left as they spotted the potential danger in the situation.

It's always the one you least suspect, and that's why you lost your job as a murder detective.

If quizzes are quizzical, what are tests?

Fun fact: Smokers huddled outside offices are put there by cigarette firms to remind people that smoking is very cool indeed.

'This time last year, we'll be millionaires.' – Del Boy invents a time machine.

Tip: Spend all day chopping onions, in case anything sad happens. You don't want people thinking you're emotionally unstable.

Say what you like about the Tartan Army, they know how to keep themselves in check.

Did you hear about the celebrity murderer? He was shooting for the stars.

Never trust an atom. They make up everything.

Every time I let my phone run out of battery, I remember why I'm no longer allowed to have pets.

When I was young I was scared of the dark. Now when I see my electricity bill I'm scared of the lights.

Whenever someone says universal healthcare is a bad idea, I just stab them in the face and say, 'Good luck paying for that.'

April Fool's Day: The day our newspapers try to fool readers by sneaking in a well-researched, factually accurate story.

If I ever go into politics, I'll call my party the Pyjama Party because who wouldn't vote for a Pyjama Party?

So I met this gangster who pulls up the back of people's pants. It was Wedgie Kray.

What's a tree's favourite drink? Root beer.

Do you know what the Queen's father was called? King.

I'm going to Rio de Janeiro to see if I can find Jesus. I've heard he's pretty big over there.

1. Pretend DVD commentary is people talking in cinema. 2. Yell SHUT UP! 3. Switch off commentary. 4. Feel like a tough guy when talking stops.

Snowmen are the polar opposites of fair-weather friends.

My ability to speak a bit of Latin is always at the top of my Curriculum Vitae.

Secretary to boss: 'Excuse me, sir, but the Invisible Man is waiting outside.' Boss: 'Tell him I can't see him.'

A man turns to his co-workers and says, 'I feel like punching the boss in the face again.' 'What d'you mean "again"?' asks one of his colleagues. 'I felt like punching him yesterday,' says the man.

Two lions are walking down the aisle of a supermarket. One turns to the other and says, 'Quiet in here today, isn't it?'

A man goes into a pet shop and sees a duck tap-dancing on an upturned flowerpot. The man buys the duck for a fiver and takes it home. Next day he rings up the pet shop to complain. 'This duck has been sitting on my kitchen table for hours,' says the man. 'It hasn't danced a single step.' The pet shop owner replies, 'Did you remember to light the candle under the flowerpot?'

I have a date tonight … with my bed. We're totally gonna sleep together.

A family is like a hand, and the middle child is very much the middle finger.

Did you hear about the butcher who backed into the meat grinder? He got behind in his work.

My paper aeroplane won't fly. It's completely stationery.

Why is being in the military like a blow job? The closer you get to discharge, the better you feel.

Sadly, most pantomime horses are real people who were actually eaten by horses.

What did the candle say to the other candle? 'I'm going out tonight.'

Just saw a bottle of Smart Water was £2. Drank from a fountain like an idiot.

Why did the hipster burn his tongue? Because he ate his food before it was cool.

'OMD!' – Jesus.

I had a bit of a lazy day sitting in my underpants looking for jobs online. My boss was furious.

Why are babies good at football? Because they dribble.

Nobody lies on their deathbed wishing they'd spent more time in the office, just that they'd stolen more stationery and sold it on.

Imagine looking in the mirror and not singing 'The Eye of the Tiger' at least twice. You can't, it's impossible.

I've woken up looking like a Channel 5 production schedule.

I've tried yoga, but I find stress less boring.

What's the cheapest kind of meat? Deer balls, they're under a buck.

If you get nervous on your first day as an erotic photographer, just picture them naked.

My wife told me she didn't want me to make a big fuss over her fortieth birthday. I didn't. She bloody did, though.

Pretty sure snakes only evolved into venomous man-eaters because people kept making fun of their lisps.

When everything's coming your way, you're in the wrong lane.

Everyone has their own reason for waking up in the morning. Mine is because the vodka wore off.

I was going have my teeth whitened, but then I said screw that, I'll just get a tan instead.

I had a strange time last night. First my blind date didn't turn up, then some woman walked in, gave me a weird look and left the restaurant.

What did the computer screen say to the keyboard after it went for a ride? That was a hard drive.

'Let's get out there and show them what we're made of!' – Biology teachers.

My friend just called me saying they've had their first child, 8lb 2oz. Stupid name for a baby if you ask me.

Throughout our marriage, my wife has always stood by my side. She's had to. We've only got one chair.

I hate how homeless people shake their coin cups at me. I get it. No need to gloat that they make more money than me.

A lawyer is someone who writes an eighty-page document and calls it a brief.

I had the right to remain silent, but I didn't have the ability.

A ticker-tape reception of losing lottery tickets is a fun way to show your landlord how close you were to paying this month's rent.

I know a guy who called up the Home Shopping Network. They said, 'Can I help you?' and he said, 'No, I'm just looking.'

I cooked for my wife's parents. As I handed out the rare-cooked steak her father said, 'I like it well done.' I said, 'Thanks, that means a lot.'

My uncle would always say, 'Pick a card, any card.' He was the most impatient Clinton's employee ever.

I once dated this girl who was so beautiful, when I took her home in a taxi I could hardly keep my eyes on the meter.

Get rich or die trying. Or buy a good life insurance policy and do both.

My hobby recreating aerial dogfights is really expensive. You're looking at between eighty and ninety helium-filled balloons just to lift a pit bull.

My book club reads wine labels.

Have you seen Stevie Wonder's new house? No? Well, it's really nice.

Avoid getting out of bed on the wrong side by never getting out of bed.

Now that I'm older, my memory is a mighty fortress. Nothing penetrates it.

Can't believe it's a whole year since I started seeing a psychiatrist. Seems like only yesterday that my pet elephant Raymond suggested it.

'Antique': A magic word that makes something old and useless suddenly priceless.

Why is divorce so expensive? Because it's worth it.

I've finally found something my girlfriend's bum doesn't look big in: the distance.

My phone is my watch, camera, iPod, torch, calculator, mailbox and so much more.

I should confront my shyness, but I never will. I hate confrontation.

A psychiatrist is a person who will give you expensive answers that you can get from your wife for free.

Just had a hand job from an eighteen-year-old prostitute. Best pro teen shake ever.

What's brown and sticky? A stick.

Caller ID should be more detailed: 'Wants help moving', 'Going to whine', 'Will ask to borrow money'.

When I was born, I was so shocked I didn't talk for a year and a half.

My cat went completely insane when I told him he was adopted. I spelled it out with a laser pointer.

This bloke said, 'My dog doesn't eat meat.' I asked, 'Why not?' He said, 'We don't give him any.'

Intelligence is like underwear. It's important that you have it but there's no need to show it off.

My parents say it's their house, but when it's time to clean it magically becomes my house too.

Life is the original limited-time offer.

'It's strange, isn't it? You stand in the middle of a library and go 'aaaaarrrrgghhhh!' and everyone just stares at you. But you do the same thing on an aeroplane and everyone joins in.

Laugh and the world laughs with you. A fake laugh, in most cases.

What's Whitney Houston's favourite type of co-ordination? HAND-EEEEEYYYYYYYYEEEEEEEEEE

Why does the Easter Bunny hide eggs? He doesn't want anyone knowing he's been shagging the chickens.

Sixty per cent of pit bull attacks occur between tying the bandana around its neck and putting the sunglasses on its face.

Imagine unpeeling a banana and not pretending you're unzipping a rescued swimmer's wetsuit to help him breathe.

Well, well, well … Welcome to stutter class.

My superpower is being able to stop even the most basic piece of technology from working.

Two Eskimos sitting in a kayak were chilly. But when they lit a fire in the craft, it sank, proving once and for all that you can't have your kayak and heat it.

I'd kill for a Nobel Peace Prize.

Why do bicycles fall over? Because they are two-tyred.

My New Year's resolutions are: 1. Stop making lists. B. Be more consistent. 7. Learn to count.

A man of thirty was talking to his girlfriend. 'I've been asked to get married hundreds of times,' he said. 'Oh!' replied his girlfriend, rather astonished. 'Who by?' 'My parents.'

'Doctor, doctor, what's the bad news?' 'We cut off the wrong leg. But the good news is that your bad leg is getting better.'

At the cocktail party, one woman said to another, 'Aren't you wearing your wedding ring on the wrong finger?' The other replied, 'Yes, I am. I married the wrong man.'

A salesman, tired of his job, gives it up to become a policeman. Several months later a friend asks him how he likes it. 'Well,' he replies. 'The pay is good and the hours aren't bad, but what I like best is that the customer is always wrong.'

Why are there no Irish lawyers? They can't pass the bar.

People say that age is just a state of mind. I say it's more about the state of your body.

Heat makes things expand. So I'm not overweight, I'm just a little too warm.

New parent idea: 1. Take pictures of you pulling baby out of spacecraft in forest. 2. Hide pictures in attic for kid to find when he's ten.

Whatever my obituary says, I just hope it's not 'He is survived by his internet history.'

MURDER ON THE DANCEFLOOR: Police say the guilty feet have got no rhythm.

My wife Dorothy is threatening to run off due to my obsession with Morse code. I begged her, 'Please don't dash Dot.'

A dyslexic walks into a bra shop, purchases a bra and leaves. Because they can still live an everyday life without constant confusion.

The worst part of winning the lottery would be no longer resenting your most successful friends.

It is not hard to meet expenses, they're everywhere.

I've never been skydiving, but I've zoomed in on Google Earth really, really fast.

I thought I'd become a wallpaper stripper but I'd just scrape a living.

Don't get me wrong, I'm glad slavery was abolished. I just don't understand why marriage is still legal.

1. Give birth to identical twins. 2. Keep one completely secret for years. 3. Send both to alcoholic uncle's intervention.

I met Barack Obama and said, 'My dad says you're spying on us all.' He said, 'He's not your dad.'

That awkward moment when Pinocchio and Voldemort meet.

As my son's hearse slowly pulled off, I couldn't control myself. I shouted to him, 'Why didn't you buy a normal car like everyone else?'

The first rule, commandment, decree, edict, law and maxim of SEO Club is 'always cover your bases'.

Amelia Earhart, Lord Lucan and Waldo walk into a bar, never to be seen again.

Why did the belt go to jail? It held up a pair of pants.

What did one saggy boob say to the other? We better get some support or people are going to think we're nuts.

One morning I shot an elephant in my pyjamas. How he got into my pyjamas I'll never know.

What did the banana say to the vibrator? 'Why are *you* shaking? She's going to eat me!'

The secret to success is knowing who to blame for your failures.

Only dull people are brilliant at breakfast.

I poured spot remover on my dog. Now he's gone.

Did you hear about the robbery last night? Two clothes pins held up a pair of pants.

The world's tallest man has died. He leaves some very big shoes to fill.

If at first you don't succeed, skydiving is not for you.

I knew a hypochondriac who wouldn't visit the Dead Sea until he found out what it died of.

What do baby apes sleep in? Apricots.

What does it take to please an Amish woman? Two Mennonite.

What does one bucket say to the other? 'I'm feeling pale today.'

The life expectancy of goldfish is short because they have terrible memories, forget how to swim and drown. So sad.

I went to buy a watch, and the man in the shop said, 'Analogue?' I said, 'No, just a watch.'

A wealthy man was having an affair with an Italian woman for several years. One night, during one of their rendezvous, she confided in him that she was pregnant. Not wanting to ruin his reputation or marriage, he paid her a large sum of money if she would go to Italy to have the child. If she stayed in Italy, he would also provide child support until the child turned eighteen. She agreed, but wondered how he would know when the baby was born. To keep it discreet, he told her to send him a postcard with 'Spaghetti' written on it. He would then arrange for child support. One day, several months later, he came home to his confused wife. 'Darling,' she said, 'you received a very strange postcard today.' 'Oh, just give it to me and I'll explain it later,' he said. The wife obeyed and watched as her husband read the card, turned white and fainted. On it was written, 'Spaghetti, Spaghetti, Spaghetti. Two with meatballs, one without.'

A young husband with an inferiority complex insisted he was just a little pebble on a vast beach. The marriage counsellor, trying to be creative, told him, 'If you want to save your marriage, you'd better be a little boulder.'

So now Findus have withdrawn their products because of horse meat contamination ... Shame, I really liked their spaghetti bologneighs.

If Barbie is so popular, then why do you have to buy her friends?

I'd like to give valentines the red card.

What do you call a cow that can play a musical instrument? A moo-sician.

My wife made me join a bridge club. I jump off next Tuesday.

Still haven't slept since I discovered Michael J. Fox's middle name is Andrew.

My parents accused me of being a liar. I looked them straight in the eye and said, 'Tooth Fairy, Santa Claus and the Easter Bunny.'

Finally found my wife's G-spot when I grabbed the handle of the vacuum cleaner.

I almost had a psychic girlfriend but she left me before we met.

A disaster is when your country has an obesity epidemic and a skinny jeans fad.

Textaphrenia – thinking you've heard or felt a new text message vibration when there is no message.

I cleaned the attic with the wife the other day. Now I can't get the cobwebs out of her hair.

The only thing worse than a room full of people wearing sunglasses is the fear that not one of them is secretly staring at me.

When I die I want my coffin to be made of onions. My family don't love me very much.

'Welcome to Hell' is a nice start, but there's a lot more to be done before Hell becomes a mainstream holiday destination.

The only 'B' word you should call a girl is beautiful. Bitches love being called beautiful.

We all think we're pretty smart until we try to turn on someone else's shower.

I'm paranoid *and* needy: I think people are talking about me, but not as much as I'd like.

Blue birds often nest in weeping willows just for a sense of perspective.

What did one butt cheek say to the other butt cheek? If we stick together, we can stop this shit.

Two little boys came home with a football. 'Where did you get that from?' asks their mother. 'We found it,' they say. 'Are you absolutely sure it was lost?' says Mum. 'Yes,' say the kids. 'We saw the people looking for it.'

A man walks into a psychiatrist's office dressed in a tutu, a diving mask and flippers. 'Doctor,' he says. 'I'm worried about my brother.'

An old man is in the street shouting into thin air. 'Why he's doing that?' asks a passer-by. 'That's old Mr Fosdyke,' says a woman. 'But he's just talking to himself again.' 'So why is he shouting?' asks the passer-by. The woman replies, 'He has to. He's deaf.'

A man walks into a bar with a giraffe and they proceed to get blitzed. The giraffe drinks so much it passes out on the floor. The man gets up and heads for the door to leave when the bartender yells, 'Hey! You can't leave that lyin' there!' The drunk replies, 'That's not a lion! It's a giraffe.'

A man went to a new barber and was horrified to find that a trim would be £20. 'But I'm practically bald,' he says. 'How can it cost £20?' 'To be honest, the cut is only £5. The other £15 is a search fee.'

Two fish in a tank – one says to the other, 'Can you drive this thing?'

Why did the boy put candy under his pillow? Because he wanted sweet dreams.

Why don't Italians like Jehovah's Witnesses? Italians don't like any witnesses.

Bring excitement to a stranger's life by crashing into their parked car and leaving a lottery ticket rather than insurance details.

It's often a very short step from self-discovery to self-harm.

I wish I partied as much as my neighbour's dog did. He's had a lampshade on his head for like two weeks straight now.

I gave my son a pocket knife and the cry-baby cut himself. So I'm dying his hair black and disguising him as an emo kid before his mum gets home.

As I handed my mum her sixtieth birthday card today she said, 'One would've been enough.'

How do you embarrass an archaeologist? Give him a used tampon and ask him which period it came from.

What makes the calendar seem so popular? It has a lot of dates.

When a girl says she has experimented with girls, that does not necessarily mean she's bi. She may just be an evil scientist.

Anything unrelated to elephants is irrelephants.

My party trick of dressing up as Mr Motivator and running directly behind people on a treadmill is underappreciated to say the very least.

As a child, my mother cleaned my face with her spit. It was like I was raised by cats.

What would Shakespeare be doing if he was alive today? Shouting and scratching at the lid on his coffin.

When I went to India for my summer holidays, I asked my doctor how I could avoid getting a disease from biting insects. He just told me not to bite any.

Did you hear about the dwarf psychic who escaped from prison? The newspaper headline read, 'Small medium at large'.

What is the difference between a clarinet and an onion? Nobody cries when you chop a clarinet into little pieces.

People ask you to bring the weather back from your holiday, then get all silly when you pour gallons of Cornish rain on their desks. Idiots.

My ex-girlfriend used to love coming home to find me naked on her bed. Now she calls the police.

Breasts are like beer. Men may state a preference, but we'll take whatever's on tap.

People who say smoking destroys your sense of taste are right. My uncle smoked for years and now he wears sandals and reads the *Daily Mail*.

My friend told me he was going to a fancy-dress party as a Cornish island. I said to him, 'Don't be Scilly.'

I'm the type of person who gains weight just by *looking* at the pie that I'm finishing.

I'm not saying my dad didn't love me, but he did like to watch my birth video backwards.

Setting your watch five minutes fast is a cool way to make unnecessary arithmetic a regular part of your day.

Once there was a family called the Biggers. There was Mr Bigger, Mrs Bigger and their son. Who was bigger, Mr Bigger or his son? His son, because he's a little Bigger!

Table football is a fun way to pretend you're barbecuing small people on a skewer.

What did the hard-boiled egg say to the boiling water? I can't get a hard-on because I was just laid.

When a bird lands safely after a particularly turbulent flight, all the worms in its tummy break into loud, spontaneous applause.

That awkward moment when a zombie is looking for brains and it walks right past you.

A man came round in hospital after a serious accident. He shouted, 'Doctor, doctor, I can't feel my legs!' The doctor replied, 'I know you can't, I had to amputate your arms.'

My family abandoned me, my ex-girlfriend took everything I own, and my children hate me, all because of my constant optimism. Still, could be worse.

If I wanted your opinion ... Oh, never mind, we both know that's just ridiculous.

What is a boxer's favourite drink? Punch.

I don't have a problem with caffeine. I have a problem without caffeine.

My wife put a bikini snap from our summer holiday as her profile picture on Facebook. She's just had a friend request from Weight Watchers.

I like children, really, I do. But I don't think I could eat a whole one.

What is a vagina? The box a penis comes in.

Don't get me wrong, I'm grateful to have a job. I just wish it wasn't THIS job.

I think the reason my wife and I get along so well is that we share a sense of humour. Well, I mean we have to, since she doesn't have one.

A relationship without trust is like having a phone with no service. And what do you do with a phone with no service? You play games.

Why do banks lock their pens to the desk? If I'm trusting you with my money, don't you think you can trust me with your pen?

I once fell in love with an escape artist. She was the one that got away.

Traffic jams are much more fun if you pretend they're staring contests, because the car in front of you always loses.

What's in the middle of nowhere? The letter H.

My wife and I are a fastidious couple. I'm fast, she's tedious.

What has legs but can't walk? A bed.

What do a toilet, a clitoris and an anniversary have in common? Men usually miss all three.

I am always right even when I am right about being wrong.

My wife left me because of my obsession with Linkin Park. But in the end, it doesn't even matter.

Right now I'm having amnesia and déjà vu at the same time. I think I've forgotten this before.

The fact that Michael Jackson had to ask Annie if she was OK nearly 100 times in four minutes makes me think she probably wasn't OK.

I got sacked from my job as a bingo caller the other day. Apparently 'a meal for two with a terrible view' isn't the best way to announce number 69.

I went to give my boss a high five today during a meeting, but he swerved it ... so I turned it into a handstand to avoid looking stupid.

'What do we want?!' 'An existential crisis!' 'Why do we want it?'

It's so sad that all the photos on the wall in the barber's are of men the barber once loved but is no longer allowed to go near.

I was reading this book the other day, *The History of Glue*. I couldn't put it down.

Make your own snooker ball by sucking a bowling ball for several hundred years.

Why did the boy take a ladder to school? He wanted to go to high school.

My pet mouse Elvis has just died. He was caught in a trap.

'I'll be with you every step of the way.' – Friend/Stalker.

Animals may be our friends. But they won't pick you up at the airport.

Don't think of today as another day wasted, think of it as another day closer to *Police Academy 8*.

I got this really cute girl's number today. I'm starting to think I should cause car accidents more often.

Nothing has ever disappointed me quite so much as discovering that Chalk Farm isn't a farm made out of chalk.

How did Ben Franklin feel after discovering electricity? Shocked.

People who enjoy the sunshine without a moment's thought for the nation's snowmen are the worst people alive.

What happened when the monster ate the electric company? He was in shock for a week.

What's the worst thing your wife can say during sex? 'Honey, I'm home.'

I was taught by a cross-eyed teacher. She couldn't control her pupils.

What do you do with 365 used condoms? Roll them up into a tyre and call it a Goodyear.

I can't believe our four-year-old son is already looking at porn online! I said to my wife when she checked the internet history.

It's so sad when you remember that 'My name is Hartley. J. R. Hartley' was just a confused old man doing his James Bond impression.

It's predicted that by 2025 you'll be no more than six feet away from an ex-Chelsea manager at any time.

Of all the possible utensils that could have been invented to eat rice with, how did two sticks win out?

Fun fact: A modern-day remake of *The Boy Who Cried Wolf* would feature a health and safety officer obsessed with fire drills.

What's the difference between roast beef and pea soup? Anyone can roast beef.

It doesn't matter if you win or lose, it matters if I win or lose.

A bird flying with worms dangling from its mouth looks like a low-budget remake of *Snakes on a Plane*.

Once I put on my headphones, my life becomes a music video.

What does a necrophiliac get at a funeral? Mourning wood.

I have my steak so rare that it helps me eat the salad.

Seventy-five per cent of my life is a lie.

My girlfriend cried for hours at our wedding. I wish I could have been there to see it.

'I'll deal with you in my office,' said my headmaster when I got caught selling drugs at school. I sold him a half-ounce.

Slept like a baby last night. Woke up every two hours, screaming.

To be sure of hitting the target, shoot first and call whatever you hit the target.

'Nobody's perfect.' – Nobody's mother.

I was taught how to get on planes at boarding school.

The police station toilet was stolen. They have nothing to go on.

Iris, do you like anagrams?

I've designed a plane made entirely from rubber, so that when it crashes, it bounces. It's a Boing 747.

Breaking news: Bears are NOT more scared of you than you are of them. Finding out the hard way here.

The Energizer Bunny got arrested. He was charged with battery.

'I'm sorry, you're breaking up' is a good thing to say when your girlfriend phones you to end the relationship.

I went to the doctors with a jelly and custard stuck in my ears. He asked, 'What seems to be the problem?' So I said, 'I'm a trifle deaf.'

After Monday and Tuesday, even the calendar says W T F.

A man was driving in his car and got a call from his wife on his cell phone. She was really frantic and yelled, 'I just heard on the news that there is a car going the wrong way on the highway! Be careful!' He replied, 'Honey, there isn't just one, there are hundreds of them!'

'Knock, knock.' 'Who's there?' 'Luke.' 'Luke who?' 'Luke through the keyhole, then you'll see who.'

I said to my doctor, 'I keep thinking I'm a pair of curtains.' And the doctor said, 'For heaven's sake, man, pull yourself together.'

Update: The combined amount of time I've spent avoiding people in supermarkets now stands at 17 days, 9 hours and 15 minutes.

How long do you have to work at KFC before they make you a colonel?

I always test psychics with a knock-knock joke. If they say 'Who's there?' I get up and leave.

I've just bought a car with 'Stop Start' technology. And next to those two pedals is the clutch.

Sadly, most 'shark attacks' are actually just well-meaning sharks trying to carry out-of-their-depth swimmers to safety.

A lorry-load of tortoises crashed into a trainload of terrapins. What a turtle disaster.

Two girls wear the same shirt: 'She copied my style!' Two guys wear the same shirt: 'BRO!'

I'm pitching a kids' version of *Snakes on a Plane*. It's called *The Eels on the Bus*.

Insanity does not run in my family. It strolls through, taking its time and getting to know each one of us personally.

'I don't know who you are, but I will find you, and I will kill you.' And that was how I lost my job as a hostage negotiator on the first day.

I'm walking on sunshine, wooah! I'm walking on sunshine, wooah! I'm – JESUS CHRIST MY FEET ARE BURNING!

People will believe anything if you whisper it.

Why did the tree get a computer? To log on.

What should you do if you see a spaceman? Park in it, man.

I never knew what happiness was until I got married … and then it was too late.

How many mice does it take to screw in a light bulb? Only two, but they have to be really small light bulbs.

Two aerials meet on a roof, fall in love, get married. The ceremony was rubbish but the reception was brilliant.

A relationship is the period of time between 'I love you' and 'everything you do pisses me off'.

If you watch *The Shawshank Redemption* backwards, it's about two guys sitting on a beach, dreaming of being somewhere with a bit more shade.

Why did the footballer bring a rope to the game? Because he wanted to tie the score.

I'm pushing sixty. That's enough exercise for me.

What do you get if you fire a flamethrower down a rabbit hole? Hot cross bunnies.

I went to the doctor's the other day, and he said, 'Go to Bournemouth, it's great for flu.' So I went – and I got it.

Sometimes I wrestle with my inner demons. Other times, we just hug.

What's the definition of mixed emotions? When you see your mother-in-law backing off a cliff in your new car.

The first rule of Chinese Whispers Club is: don't talk about Tiny Whiskers Grub.

The more police mugshots I see, the more I think police stations should have a hair and make-up department.

What's the best time to go to the dentist? Tooth-hurty.

I saw a man sleeping in the doorway of HMV. So I snuggled in next to him. They must have a bloody good sale on tomorrow.

'I'm sick and tired of living a lie!' – Chameleon resignation letter.

'Dad, did you know in some countries men don't know their wives till after they get married?' 'It's like that in every country, son.'

I've been thinking about trying some cosmetic surgery. All of my family and friends recognise me.

What did the cannibal do after he dumped his girlfriend? Washed his hands.

I swam the English Channel once. 'But a lot of people have swum the Channel.' Lengthwise?

I've seen the photos from Mars and I'm amazed that Curiosity could find wireless coverage.

What two things can you not have for breakfast? Lunch and dinner.

Lollipop ladies should marry ice-cream men and have hundreds and thousands of babies.

Why did the girl smear peanut butter on the road? To go with the traffic jam.

They say you'll find love in the unlikeliest places, but I've been in the Sahara for a week now and I'm not convinced. Also, SEND WATER.

Silence is golden. Unless you have a toddler. Then, silence is just suspicious.

Don't accuse me of going through a mid-life crisis. I've been in crisis mode from day one.

My doctor said I should bathe in milk but I couldn't fit into the bottle.

What do you call a judge with no balls? Justice Prick.

Minnie told Mickey that she wanted a divorce. Mickey said, 'Are you crazy?' She said, 'No, I'm fucking Goofy.'

So sad when you think you've met the perfect girl and then she puts a coffee-soaked spoon in the sugar bowl and you have to say goodbye.

It's so sad how before umbrellas were invented people had to walk around in the rain carrying their largest child above their head.

If another day goes by without a Matthew, Mark, Luke and John forming a boy band called New Testament, I'm giving up on everything.

NASA would be a lot more popular if once in a while they'd fight some Klingons.

I've written a book on being made unemployed. Ironically, it ends on page 45.

Don't be racist, be like Super Mario. He's an Italian plumber, created by Japanese people, who speaks English, and looks like a Mexican.

Either I've gained a few pounds or there's a bowl of jelly following me.

Someone threw NaCl at me. I said, 'Hey, that's a salt!'

To celebrate World Book Day I've just killed a mocking-bird and I'm now going for a big sleep.

I can't believe people keep asking me to name my favourite fruit, it's bananas!

Somewhere in the world, a woman gives birth to a child every minute. We have to find this woman and stop her.

Two cannibals are having dinner. 'Your wife makes a great roast,' says one. 'I know,' says the other, 'but I'm going to miss her.'

Did you hear about the author who changed his name to 'Biro'? He wanted a pen name.

What goes 'tick, tock, woof'? A watch dog.

If you see lions sleeping at the zoo, wake them up! They may be undercover police pretending to be lions. They'll thank you if they are.

I'm quick to jump to confusion.

What do skid marks on the toilet bowl and girlfriends have in common? They're both easy to piss off.

Imagine being a doctor and not saying 'I'm just going to listen to Heart FM' every time you use a stethoscope.

I got fired from my job at Pepsi. I tested positive for Coke.

Be the life and soul of the party by drinking alone in a cemetery.

Murder, She Wrote is my favourite TV show about an elderly serial killer who travels the world framing innocent people for her awful crimes.

'Remember the scene in *Anaconda* when Jon Voight's eaten then regurgitated by a giant snake?' would be a cool start to a retirement speech.

It's so sad when someone wins the lottery and then gets to the bank to find those giant cheques aren't actually valid.

The 50-metre heatstroke is probably the toughest of all swimming events.

Well, I was bullied at school, called all kinds of different names. But one day I turned to my bullies and said, 'Sticks and stones may break my bones but names will never hurt me', and it worked! From there on it was sticks and stones all the way.

If the whole world smoked a joint at the same time, there would be world peace for at least two hours. Followed by a global food shortage.

Dora the Internet Explorer would often crash before arriving at her destination.

Politicians and nappies have one thing in common; they should both be changed regularly, and for the same reason.

I didn't fight my way to the top of the food chain to be a vegetarian.

It doesn't take much to make a woman happy. However, it takes even less to make her mad.

Sometimes I wake up grumpy. Other times, I let her sleep.

Foxes keeping me awake with their mating noises is bad enough, but going through my bins and laughing at my bank statements is just rude.

Roses are red, that much is true, but violets are purple, not bloody blue.

Maybe middle fingers are so angry because their next-door neighbour has a much better chance of getting married.

Wow, you dress up like the Grim Reaper *one* time and they never let you back into this nursing home.

I've just designed new letterheads for a plastic surgeon. The new ones read: 'If life gives you lemons, a simple operation can give you melons.'

My wife went overseas. My friend asked, 'Jamaica?' I said, 'No, she went of her own accord.'

Some things are better left unsaid. If only I could determine which things.

I feel for Olympic football players. I know what it's like to try to score for ninety minutes and get nowhere.

Apparently it's Suicide Awareness Day. I wasn't sure what that entails, so I've just been looking up when walking past tall buildings.

The worst thing about having more money than sense is the fact I don't have very much money.

'Terminally ill man loses right to die court battle.' He may have lost the battle but something tells me he'll eventually win the war.

What did the sign on the door of the whorehouse say? 'Beat it, we're closed.'

The trouble with jogging is, by the time you realise you're not in shape, it's too far to walk back.

You know your childhood is over when you fall asleep on the sofa and wake up on the sofa.

The worst part of being a sommelier is that the harder you work, the harder it gets to pronounce your job title.

What do you call an obese psychic? A four-chin teller.

I bought my wife a wooden leg for Christmas. It wasn't her main present, just a stocking filler.

My most extraordinary feat turns out to be a twist of fate.

Warning: The consumption of beer may make you think you are whispering when you are not.

Why did the football coach go to the bank? To get his quarterback.

People who live in glass houses only have themselves to blame if the glass ceiling stops them getting to the top.

I don't just have issues; I have a subscription.

I'll see your suspicious behaviour and raise you an eyebrow.

I've failed to conceal from the kids the embarrassing reality that I like to dress up in women's clothes. I'm so transparent.

Why did the news reporter go to the ice-cream parlour? Because she wanted to get a good scoop.

If I've learned one thing in my life … then the British education system has really let me down.

I had a friend who was a clown. When he died, all his friends went to the funeral in one car.

You can't fight progress. But I've noticed you can unplug a lot of it.

Convince people you're a method actor preparing for a film about a man with no friends by being a man and having no friends.

I popped into the Wonga shop next door to borrow a pen. I've got to give them seventy pens back by the end of the week.

Being told you have just sixty seconds left to live is the worst last-minute deal ever.

I went to a record store, they said they specialised in hard-to-find records. Nothing was alphabetised.

I've just realised how evil tree houses really are: it's like killing someone and nailing him to his mate.

Such a missed opportunity that the highest-ranked belt you can get in karate isn't pink and glittery.

An aspiring young actor asks his girlfriend's father if he can have her hand in marriage. The father says, 'I would never let my daughter marry an actor.' The actor replies, 'Sir, I think you may change your mind if you see me perform. Won't you at least come and see the play?' So the father goes to see the play and calls the actor the next day. 'You were right. I did change my mind. Go ahead and marry my daughter. You're certainly no actor.'

Last year the children and I had a lot of fun on holiday burying my husband in the sand on the beach. Next year we might go back and dig him up.

This guy walks into a bar with a really great shirt on. The bartender goes, 'Where'd you get the great shirt, mate?' The man replies, 'David Jones.' This second guy walks into the bar with really good trousers on and the bartender goes, 'Where'd you get those great trousers, mate?' The man replies, 'David Jones.' This third guy walks into the bar with really great socks and shoes on. The bartender goes, 'Where'd you get those great socks and shoes, mate?' The man replies, 'David Jones.' Then this fourth guy runs in naked and the bartender goes, 'Who the hell are you, mate?' And the naked guy says, 'I'm David Jones!'

'Haven't I seen your face before?' a judge demanded, looking down at the defendant. 'You have, Your Honour,' the man answered hopefully. 'I gave your son violin lessons last winter.' 'Ah yes,' recalled the judge. 'Twenty years!'

Two peanuts walk into a rather rough bar, not looking for any trouble. Unfortunately, one was a salted.

It's nothing special, but I can shrug in eight different languages.

Whenever I say 'never again,' I always do it again.

Why can't Jesus eat M&Ms? Because he has holes in his hands.

Why did the opera singer go sailing? Because she wanted to hit the high Cs.

My exercise programme consists of having a lot of stairs in my house and forgetting things.

Just so you know, not every hot tip for Cheltenham you get from a drunk bloke in the pub will actually win.

Fun fact: Before Twitter, people only watched TV shows they actually liked.

Of course my password's insecure. So would you be if people replaced you every six months.

Why can't you tell a joke on an ice rink? Because it might crack up.

When I was in the army, once the sergeant said to me: 'What does surrender mean?' I said: 'I give up.'

I thought I knew the way to a woman's heart, but I got lost outside the pericardium and now I'm too embarrassed to ask for directions.

What kind of crisps fly? Plane ones.

My friend asked, 'What's the secret to your happy marriage?' I replied, 'Chemistry. I'm on Valium and the wife's on Prozac.'

I could snap at any moment. Seriously, with either hand.

One time, this guy handed me a picture of him. He said, 'Here's a picture of me when I was younger.' Every picture is of you when you were younger.

At my age, only three things can make me go running. When someone yells, 'Fire!', 'Free food!', or 'The free food's on fire!'

In what school do you learn how to greet people? High school.

'I forgot, I've got a doctor's appointment tomorrow.' 'Just cancel it. Tell them you're sick.'

Why did the minus sign run for office? To make a difference.

What has little balls and screws old ladies? A bingo machine.

'It's not you, it's me.' – Clever twist at the end of my screenplay *It's Not You, It's Me.*

You're never too old to smile and nod when your mum is giving advice while thinking, 'That's never gonna happen.'

The older I get, the more I suspect my dad was lying when he told me eating bananas would help me see around corners.

Pilots look up to astronauts as farther figures.

What kind of lights did Noah have on the ark? Flood lights.

Where does Friday come before Monday? In the dictionary.

Shouting 'Put your hands in the air like you just don't care!' is a fun way to bring a party atmosphere to a bank robbery.

An angry woman can pack everything she owns in an hour, but it will take her a week to pack for vacation? WOMEN.

Did you hear about the women who got wooden breast implants? A punch line would be funny here, Wooden Tit?

I wish these two tailors would get on with their fight. They've been sizing each other up for hours.

An empty browsing history is a dirty browsing history.

It's useless to hold a person to anything he says while he's in love, drunk, or running for office.

How many interns does it take to change a light bulb? Just one, I hope, and he needs to hurry up. The CEO wants another coffee.

A horse walks into a bar. The barman confuses idioms with jokes and offers him water, but can't make him drink.

How do you make an octopus laugh? Ten tickles.

Have you heard of the new movie called *Constipation*? It hasn't come out yet.

Why does every girl I like have a husband or boyfriend or girlfriend or standards?

Going from vegetarian to vegan just left me irate, on reflection.

The trouble with being punctual is that no one is there to appreciate it.

'Is your husband helping you with the baby?' 'Sure, he takes naps for the baby.'

A little girl walks into a pet shop and asks with the sweetest little lisp, 'Excuthe me, mithter, do you keep wittle wabbits?' And the shopkeeper gets down on his knees, so that he's on her level, and asks, 'Do you want a wittle white wabby or a soft and fwuffy bwack wabby or maybe one like that cute wittle bwown wabby over there?' The little girl puts her hands on her knees, leans forward and says in a quiet voice, 'I don't fink my pyfon weally giveths a thit.'

A secretary walks into her boss's office and says, 'I'm afraid I've got some bad news for you.' 'For heaven's sake,' says her boss. 'Why do you always have to bring me bad news? Try to be more positive.' 'All right,' replies the secretary. 'The good news is that you're not sterile.'

How do you make your girlfriend scream while having sex? Call her and tell her.

I don't know why hedgehogs think that rolling into a ball is a good defence mechanism. I wasn't going to kick it before.

There are some things better left unsaid. That's usually the stuff I blurt out first thing.

Either there's a family of hedgehogs in my garden or my guinea pigs have been re-enacting medieval spear battles again.

Fun fact: The McDonald's golden arches represent two nutritionists frowning.

Just noticed a sign on a pub door saying 'Guide Dogs Only'. Possibly the most exclusive pub ever.

What do a Rubix cube and a penis have in common? The more you play with it the harder it gets.

What did the light bulb say to its mother? 'I wuv you watts and watts.'

It's 2013 and the other drinks are still making jokes about ginger ale's funny hair. Unacceptable.

I have a sunny disposition. I just don't like to show it to anyone.

I often wonder what tomatoes did to make the other fruits disown them and force them to live as vegetables.

Having Barack Obama's initials must stink.

What kind of table has no legs? A multiplication table.

What is the opposite of a restaurant? A workaraunt.

I told my son that if anybody ever tries to take his lunch money at school then he should headbutt them. The silly little sod was sent home today for breaking the dinner lady's nose.

Two things I've been cursed with are a weak bladder and terrible amnesia. Still, this bottle of apple juice should take my mind off things.

Ideally the towns of Cheddar or Stilton, for example, should be twinned with a nice port, such as Honfleur in Normandy.

We got a new science teacher in school today called Mr Frankenstein ... Can't wait for assembly tomorrow.

Fun fact: An Eskimo's wife has fifty different words for no.

'I correct you, I'm just not incorrect with you.' – Pedants.

I hope I live a long life. There are so many things I haven't tried and failed at yet.

The definition of insanity is doing the same thing over and over again and not marrying someone who realises just how sexy OCD can be.

Did you see the Broadway musical about the dictionary? It's a play on words.

What did the letter O say to Q? 'Dude, your dick is hanging out.'

Why is it that when someone tells you that there are over a billion stars in the universe, you believe them, but if they tell you there is wet paint somewhere, you have to touch it to make sure?

Imagine *not* wearing a cape and listening to 'The Sorcerer's Apprentice' every time you do the housework.

I don't have time to discuss all the lies in your name, jellyfishes.

As students return to campus, remember, college is a fountain of knowledge and students are there to drink.

Not saying I'm lonely, but sometimes I just drive around pretending the sat-nav is a close friend directing me to a party.

'And the rest is history.' – Me, after having a rest.

'Suicide is not the answer,' I said to my mate. But he insisted it was, and we lost the quiz by one point.

What's the tallest building in the world? The library, because it has the most stories.

Imagine sharpening a pencil and not pretending it's a tall enemy you've always wanted to torture and make shorter at the same time.

A letter G walks into a hexadecimal bar. The barman says, 'Why the wrong base?'

I saw a man at the beach yelling. 'Help, shark! Help!' I just laughed. I knew that shark wasn't going to help him.

'STOP MAKING FOOLS OUT OF US!' – Gooseberries.

I threw some snow at my wife but she didn't catch my drift.

I hate it when you call shotgun but the cops still throw you in the back.

Warning: Objects in profile pictures are not as pretty as they appear.

I'm not saying not to trust the internet, but there's an alarming discrepancy between the number of iPads I've won and the number of iPads I own.

'Why do only the good die young?' is a fun question to ask your grandparents.

Just so you know, kissing someone mid-sentence works better in films than when a bus conductor is asking why you don't have a valid ticket.

I bet you I could stop gambling.

I made a rose-tinted spectacle of myself last night. Probably wasn't as funny as I remember it.

Why did the student eat her homework? Because the teacher said it was a piece of cake.

You know, I wasn't convinced about that complicated political issue until I saw your overly simplified bumper sticker.

If you are an American in the living room, what are you in the bathroom? European.

I met this bloke with a didgeridoo and he was playing 'Dancing Queen' on it. I thought, 'That's Aboriginal.'

My wife does her own decorating, but she overdoes it. The other day I opened the fridge and there was a lampshade on the light.

If you say 'How are you?' and I say 'Fine – you?' and you say 'Fine – you?' it's almost like you're not concentrating and don't really care.

Were there any great men born in this town? No, only little babies.

Which US state abbreviation is the best? I'm not sure, but Oklahoma's is OK.

Before telling interviewers where you see yourself in five years' time, watch an episode of *The Jetsons* so you know what you're talking about.

His bark is worse than his bite, and that's why his dog-fighting career came to such an unfortunate end.

I'm not saying that the customer service in my bank is bad, but when I went in the other day and asked the clerk to check my balance ... she leaned over and pushed me.

An executive is interviewing a nervous young woman for a position in his company. 'If you could have a conversation with someone, living or dead, who would it be?' asks the executive. The woman replies, 'The living one.'

The defendant in one court case said that at the time the crime was committed he was in hospital, recovering from a vicious attack by a shark while swimming in the sea. He therefore had a water-bite alibi.

'Doctor, Doctor! Every time I eat fruit I get this strange urge to give people all my money.' 'Would you like an apple or a banana?'

If you are trying to insult me, you are going to have to use smaller words.

Why did Isaac Newton's son know so much about gravity? The apple didn't fall far from the tree.

All evidence seems to suggest that deathbeds are a bit *too* comfortable.

How do you cut a wave in half? Use a see-saw.

I have plenty of money and would like a psychic but I'm not going to ring one. I'm just going to wait for the best one to knock on my door.

What letter can you drink? T

Maybe tortoises aren't slow. Maybe they're just remaking *Chariots of Fire*.

I know people are talking about me because my ears are burning and JESUS CHRIST, NO WONDER THEY'RE TALKING ABOUT ME, MY EARS ARE ON FIRE!

Alcohol goes in, truth comes out.

Imagine having a ceiling fan and not pretending you're in a giant, fully furnished helicopter.

What did one egg say to the other egg? 'You crack me up!'

What did the fish say when he swam into a wall? Dam.

The Tube driver's insisting I use *all* the available doors, but quite frankly I have neither the time nor the energy.

Told the doctor I thought I had athlete's foot. He looked at me and said, 'I don't think you have athlete's anything.'

How does a woman scare a gynaecologist? By becoming a ventriloquist.

Ten: Number of fingers children have. Twenty-six: Number of fingers children have when you try to put gloves on them.

'Love will set you free' is just one of the many sinister lies you're told in prison.

I hate it when people talk during the minute's silence I'm having for the fruit that has died on my desk recently.

Last night I dreamed I ate a 10lb marshmallow. When I woke up, the pillow was gone.

What can you put in a barrel to make it lighter? Holes.

The cashier told me, 'Strip down, facing me.' How was I to know she meant my debit card?

I work well with others when they leave me the hell alone.

Half an hour into *The Iron Lady* and Margaret Thatcher seems lovely. No wonder she's so fondly remembered.

Never put your superpowers on your CV. Always hold something back.

When a bird craps on my car, I like to sit outside and eat a plate of scrambled eggs, just so all the other birds know what I'm capable of.

I would never cheat in a relationship, because that would require two people to find me attractive.

'Doctor, doctor!' 'Who's there?' 'Oh, sorry ... should I have knocked?' 'Never mind. What's the problem?' 'I don't understand joke formats.'

When I was your age, internet was called television.

Did you hear about the guy with the invisible penis? He came out of nowhere.

Why is it called mooning when you're actually showing Uranus?

This pub's 'No Glasses To Be Taken Outside' sign explains both the spectacles on the bar and the people bumping into each other outside.

A dog goes into a job centre and asks for employment. 'Wow, a talking dog,' says the clerk. 'With your talent I'm sure we can find you a job in the circus.' 'The circus?' says the dog. 'What does a circus want with a plumber?'

Instructor to trainee park ranger: 'You see an enraged grizzly bear approaching a group of tourists. What steps do you take?' Park ranger: 'Large ones – in the opposite direction.'

Surgeon to patient: 'I have good news and bad news about your operation. The bad news is that it's a risky procedure and your chances of survival are 99 to one against.' 'Oh my God!' says the patient. 'So what's the good news?' The surgeon replies, 'The good news is that my last 99 patients died.'

A man asks a judge to let him off jury service. The judge says, 'But surely your firm can manage without you for a few weeks.' 'Certainly,' the man replies. 'They can manage without me altogether – and I don't want them to find out.'

What do you call a man who cries while he masturbates? A tearjerker.

Bill Gates has offered $100,000 to anyone who invents a more attractive condom. Who's going to buy a condom from a company called Microsoft?

Your hangover is the ghost of every dance move you murdered last night.

Despite the repeated false alarms, I've investigated at length and my sex is not, I repeat NOT on fire. Disappointing.

Cashiers are always checking me out.

I hate it when I plan a conversation in my head and the other person doesn't follow the script.

My mate Jim says I'm schizophrenic, which is weird, because I don't have a mate called Jim.

Why was the maths book sad? It had too many problems.

Tesco are giving treble points on your Clubcard for all burgers and petrol, starting Monday. The deal's called 'Only Fuel and Horses'.

What has a head but no body? A nail.

I hate it when people are at your house and ask 'Do you have a bathroom?' No, we crap in the garden.

How do you stop a clown from smiling? Shoot him in the face.

'Why did you swallow the coins, my boy?' 'You said it was lunch money!'

Have you been mis-sold a mail order bride?

I just made my hamster a strong coffee. I don't want him falling asleep at the wheel.

I went into this pub and I ate a ploughman's lunch. He was livid.

Why does your gynaecologist leave the room when you get undressed?

A baby's laughter is the greatest sound in the world. Unless it's 3 a.m. and you're home alone … and you don't have a baby.

How do they say 'fuck you' in Los Angeles? 'Trust me.'

I hate to be a pessimist, but I'm starting to think I might never win the EuroMillions jackpot.

I wanted to buy a train ticket to France. The agent said, 'Eurostar?' I said, 'Well, I've been on the telly, but I'm no Dean Martin.'

My bed is a magical place where I can suddenly remember everything I was supposed to do.

Great people talk about ideas. Average people talk about events. Small people talk about other people. Fools talk about the bins going out.

There are few better metaphors for life than the wooden stick outliving the delicious ice lolly.

There's no sadder sight than a room full of elephants ignoring each other.

After thirteen fun but exhausting years, I've finally stopped moving to the S Club beat.

Google: I know everything. Facebook: I know everyone. Internet: Without me, you're nothing. Electricity: Keep talking fools.

What did the blonde say when her doctor told her that she was pregnant? 'Is it mine?'

If you love someone, set them free. And then spy on them to see what they get up to when you're not together.

Just typed 'World's Sexiest Man' into Google. 58,500,000 results and not one mention of me. I hate the internet.

Pearl Jam's 'Elderly Woman behind the Counter in a Small Town' is still my favourite song about elderly women behind counters in small towns.

Why didn't the girl take the bus home? Because her mum would make her take it back.

How many ears does Spock have? Three: a right ear, a left ear, a final frontier.

In Las Vegas, they gamble everywhere. I went into a drug store for an aspirin and the girl behind the counter said, 'I'll toss you, double or nothing.' I lost. I came out with two headaches.

I am only a couple more apps from never having to speak to my husband again.

I'm planning to be spontaneous. Tomorrow.

We built this city on rock and roll. And that was fun. However, we now need to add more important things, like a post office and a library.

Keep your friends close and your enemies tied to a wardrobe, covered in glitter.

A TCP packet walks into a bar and says to the barman, 'Hello, I'd like a beer.' The barman replies, 'Hello, you'd like a beer?' 'Yes,' replies the TCP packet, 'I'd like a beer.'

The photocopier says it's 'ready to accept a new job' and now I'm thinking even machines hate Mondays.

Police officer: How high are you? Me: No, officer, it's 'Hi, how are you?'

A duck walks into a bar, the bartender says, 'What'll it be?' The duck doesn't say anything because it's a duck.

Million-dollar idea ... Take £650,068.00 to the bureau de change and ask them to change it to US dollars.

How does a Scotsman find a sheep in tall grass? Very satisfying.

The world's best gardener died last week, which is why the grass is greener on the other side.

UKIP – not so much a political party, more a *League of Gentlemen* sketch that got out of hand.

Why was the broom late? It overswept.

My parents used to read me the riot act all the time. Worst bedtime story ever.

I'm getting tired of having to write 'Sent from my iPhone' at the end of all my emails. Maybe I should just get an iPhone.

A man walks up to a house and says, 'Hello, I'm looking for the people who live here.' 'Well,' says the man at the door. 'You've come to the right place.'

Doctor to hospital patient: 'Your coughing seems to be easier this morning.' Patient: 'It should be. I've been practising all night.'

I think I have the perfect wife. Fortunately I'm not married to her.

When the famous chef was cremated the service lasted for thirty minutes at gas mark 6.

When buying an old second-hand car, always insist on getting one with a heated rear window. That way, in winter you can warm your hands while you're pushing it.

We're like two peabrains in a pod.

What do you get when you run over a goose? Goose bumps.

All my ducks are in a row, so my all-duck musical is just about ready to go.

What did the scarf say to the hat? You go on ahead, I'll hang around.

You can't become a pilot without a good altitude.

'It's curtains for you, sunshine…' is a cool thing to say before closing the curtains because the sun's getting in your eyes.

How many times have we all said, 'I'm starving, I could eat a horse.' Now we're all moaning about it.

'You're not the boss of me!' is a cool thing to say to someone who just fired you.

Why did Mickey Mouse take a trip into space? He wanted to find Pluto.

You need plenty of patients in a busy doctor's waiting room.

Hippos kill nearly 3,000 people every year, which proves even animals can be ridiculously oversensitive about their weight.

A policeman stopped me and said, 'Would you please blow into this bag, sir?' I said, 'What for, officer?' He said, 'My chips are too hot.'

All of us could take a lesson from the weather. It pays no attention to criticism.

A man walks into a bar and pauses. At the other end of the bar, there's this guy with a big orange head. Just kind of sitting there, looking into his drink. So the man asks the bartender, 'Say, what's up with the guy with the big orange head?' And the bartender says, 'It's an interesting story. Buy him a drink and maybe he'll tell it to you.' So the man walks over and introduces himself and offers to buy a round. The guy with the big orange head says, 'Yeah, I'll bet you want to know the story, huh?' To which the man replies, 'Sure, if you don't mind.' The man with the big orange head sighs and says, 'You know, I've gone over it in my mind a million times. Basically, it's like this: I was walking along the beach one day, when I stubbed my toe on something. I looked down, and there was an antique brass lamp. I picked it up and dusted it off a little – when all of a sudden this enormous genie pops out! The genie thundered, "You have released me from my ten-thousand-year imprisonment, and I am in your debt. I will grant you three wishes as a token of my gratitude."' The man at the bar is aghast. The guy with the big orange head continues: 'So I said, "Wow, OK. Well, my first wish is to be fantastically wealthy." The genie says, "Your wish is granted." And all of a sudden I have rings on my fingers and a crown on my head, and my wallet is full of money and a dozen debit cards and the deed to a mansion in the hills. I mean, I was loaded! So I said, "Amazing! OK, for my next wish, I want to be married to the most beautiful woman in the world." The genie says, "Your wish is granted." And the ocean parts, and out walks this gorgeous woman in this beautiful dress, and she takes my hand and we fall in love and the genie marries us right there. It was incredible. Then the genie booms, "You have one wish remaining."' The man with the big orange head pauses and sips his beer. He says, 'Now, you know, this may be where I went wrong. I wished for a big orange head.'

What did the grape say when it was squeezed? Nothing, it just let out a little wine.

An Irishman walks out of a bar.

A duck walks into a corner shop and says 'Give me some chapstick, put it on my bill!' But the cash register attendee doesn't speak English and cannot understand him. He does, however, question whether his God is punishing him because as all people know, ducks cannot speak, so this hallucination must be punishment for a horrid misdeed. The employee breaks down into tears and begins reciting prayers. The duck, slightly miffed, walks out, pondering why he'd need chapstick anyway, since he has no lips.

Why did the blonde get fired from the M&M factory? Repeated absences and stealing.

And the Lord said unto John, 'Come forth and receive eternal life.' But John came fifth and won a toaster.

What do you call 100 lawyers at the bottom of the ocean? A horrible boating accident.

Luke Skywalker and Darth Vader are fighting a light-saber battle when Vader says, 'I know what you're getting for Christmas.' Luke ignores him and keeps fighting, but Vader says again, 'I know what you're getting for Christmas.' Again, Luke ignores him. The battle intensifies and Vader says again, 'I know what you're getting for Christmas.' Finally, Luke has had enough. 'That's impossible! How could you possibly know?' Vader replies, 'I have felt your presents.'

A man walked into a sperm bank. The receptionist said, 'Get a load of this guy.'

This girl texted me, 'Your adorable.' I texted back, 'No, YOU'RE adorable.' Now she likes me, when all I was doing was pointing out her typo.

A woman gets on a bus with her baby. The driver says, 'Ugh, that's the ugliest baby I've ever seen!' The woman walks to the rear of the bus and sits down, fuming. She says to the man next to her, 'The driver just insulted me!' The man says, 'You go up there and tell him off. Go on, I'll hold your monkey for you.'

I went to the zoo the other day, but all I saw was a dog in a cage. It was a shih-tzu.

My mother-in-law fell down a wishing well. I was amazed, I never knew they worked.

I saw this bloke chatting up a cheetah. I thought, 'He's trying to pull a fast one.'

So I was in my car, and I was driving along, and my boss rang up, and he said, 'You've been promoted.' And I swerved. And then he rang up a second time and said, 'You've been promoted again.' And I swerved again. He rang up a third time and said, 'You're Managing Director.' And I went into a tree. And a policeman came up and said, 'What happened to you?' And I said, 'I careered off the road.'

A woman has twins and gives them up for adoption. One goes to a family in Egypt and is named Amal. The other goes to a family in Spain, who name him Juan. Years later, Juan sends a picture of himself to his mother. Upon receiving the picture, she tells her husband that she wished she also had a picture of Amal. Her husband responds, 'They're twins. If you've seen Juan, you've seen Amal.'

When Susan's boyfriend proposed, she said, 'I love the simple things in life, but I don't want one of them as a husband.'

I met a Dutch girl with inflatable shoes last week. I rang her up to arrange a date, but unfortunately she'd popped her clogs.

A priest, a rabbi and a vicar walk into a bar. The barman says, 'Is this some kind of joke?'

A sandwich walks into a bar. The barman says, 'Sorry, we don't serve food in here.'

The other day I sent my girlfriend a huge pile of snow. I rang her up. I said, 'Did you get my drift?'

A group of chess enthusiasts checked into a hotel and were standing in the lobby discussing their recent tournament victories. After about an hour, the manager came out of the office and asked them to disperse. 'But why?' they asked, as they moved off. 'Because', he said, 'I can't stand chess nuts boasting in an open foyer.'

I was in Tesco's and I saw this man and woman wrapped in a barcode. I said, 'Are you two an item?'

Two hunters are out in the woods when one of them collapses. He doesn't seem to be breathing and his eyes are glazed. The other guy whips out his phone and calls the emergency services. He gasps, 'My friend is dead! What can I do?' The operator says, 'Calm down. I can help. First, let's make sure he's dead.' There is a silence, and then a gunshot is heard. Back on the phone, the guy says, 'OK, now what?'

Sherlock Holmes and Dr Watson were going camping. They pitched their tent under the stars and went to sleep. Sometime in the middle of the night Holmes woke Watson up and said, 'Watson, look up at the sky, and tell me what you see.' Watson replied, 'I see millions and millions of stars.' Holmes said, 'And what do you deduce from that?' Watson replied, 'Well, if there are millions of stars, and if even a few of those have planets, it's quite likely there are some planets like Earth out there. And if there are a few planets like Earth out there, there might also be life.' And Holmes said, 'Watson, you idiot, it means that somebody stole our tent.'

What kind of murderer has moral fibre? A cereal killer.

My wife wanted to go to the ballet. I said, 'I'm not going to sit and watch a lot of people on their toes in long underwear.' She said, 'You don't have to. Wear your tuxedo.'

This old man was dying and he called his nephew to his bedside. He said, 'I'm leaving you all my money.' The nephew said, 'Thank you, Uncle. What can I do for you?' He said, 'Get your foot off my oxygen tube.'

In days of old, when knights were bold, the king turned to his knight and said, 'What have you been doing today?' The knight said, 'I have been robbing and pillaging on your behalf, burning the villages of your enemies in the north.' The King said, 'But I don't have any enemies in the north.' The knight said, 'I'm afraid you do now.'

This guy bought his wife a burial plot for her birthday. The following year, when he bought her nothing, she complained. He said, 'What are you complaining about? You didn't use the present I bought you last year!'

A piano tuner was called to a nightclub to tune the piano. He was at it for five hours, but the bill only came to £3. The manager said: 'Is that all? How come you worked for five hours to tune the piano and you only charge £3?' He said: 'What?'

When I was a kid, I went to a psychiatrist for one of those aptitude tests. On the desk he put a pitchfork, a wrench and a hammer and he said to the nurse, 'If he grabs the pitchfork, he'll become a farmer. If he grabs the wrench, he'll be a mechanic, and if he takes the hammer, he'll be a carpenter.' I grabbed the nurse.

The town was so dull, one day the tide went out and it never came back.

This fellow walked into a bar with a chicken under one arm and a crocodile under the other. The barman said, 'What'll you have?' He said, 'A whisky and soda.' Then the crocodile spoke up and said, 'I'll have a gin and tonic.' The barman said, 'That's amazing. I've never seen a crocodile that could talk before.' He said, 'He can't. The chicken's a ventriloquist.'

People learn something new every day. Why, just today, my wife learned that a car won't climb a telephone pole.

It wasn't easy to get us kids to eat olives. I had to start off on Martinis.

A leopard went to see a psychiatrist. He said, 'Every time I look at my wife, I see spots before my eyes.' The psychiatrist said, 'That's only natural.' The leopard said, 'But, doctor, she's a zebra.'

A man takes his Rottweiler to the vet. 'My dog is cross-eyed, is there anything you can do for him?' 'Well,' said the vet, 'let's have a look at him.' So he picks the dog up and examines his eyes, then he checks his teeth. Finally, he says, 'I'm going to have to put him down.' 'What? Because he's cross-eyed?' 'No, because he's really heavy.'

Guy goes into the doctor's. 'Doc, I've got a cricket ball stuck up my backside.' 'How's that?' 'Don't you start.'

Lawyer: Now that you have been acquitted, will you tell me truly? Did you steal the car? Client: After hearing your amazing argument in court this morning, I'm beginning to think I didn't.

'Betting on horses is a funny old game,' says a man to his friend. 'You win one day and lose the next.' The friend replies, 'So why not bet every other day?'

Two country rustics are riding a train for the first time. They've brought along a bag of apples for lunch, and, just as one bites into his apple, the train enters a long tunnel. 'Have you taken a bite out of your apple yet?' he asks. 'No,' says the other. 'Well, don't,' says the first. 'I just did and I went blind.'

The police have reported the theft of a shipment of filing cabinets, document folders and labelling machines. It is believed to have been the work of organised crime.

When I came home last night the wife complained that the cat had upset her – but she really shouldn't have eaten it in the first place.

For months a little boy had been pestering his father to take him to the zoo. Eventually, his father gave in and off they went. When they got back the boy's mother asked him if he'd had a good time. 'It was great,' replied the boy. 'And Daddy had fun too, especially when one of the animals came in at thirty to one.'

At the Three Bears' house, Daddy Bear roars, 'Who's been eating my porridge?' Baby Bear squeaks, 'Who's been eating my porridge?' And Mummy Bear snaps, 'Shut up! I haven't made the damn porridge yet. Do we have to go through this every morning?'

I'd give my right arm to be ambidextrous.

The less people know the more stubbornly they know it.

When I first went out with my girlfriend she made me lay all my cards on the table – Barclaycard, American Express...

Two elephants walk off a cliff … boom, boom!

This fella is on safari in Africa when he comes across an elephant lying on the ground, in distress. He investigates and finds a thorn in its foot. He removes it, and the elephant trots merrily away. Twenty years on, the man is standing in the street in London watching a circus procession pass by. When the elephant gets level with him, it stops, looks straight at him, reaches out with its trunk, lifts him bodily into the air, smashes him on the ground and jumps on him. It was a different elephant.

My mother was always pulling my leg. That's why one is six inches longer than the other.

Two fat blokes in a pub, one says to the other, 'Your round.' The other one says, 'So are you, you fat bastard!'

Ireland's worst air disaster occurred early this morning when a small two-seater Cessna plane crashed into a cemetery. Irish search and rescue workers have recovered 1,826 bodies so far and expect that number to climb as digging continues into the night.

I went to the doctor's. He said, 'What appears to be the problem?' I said, 'I keep having the same dream, night after night. Beautiful girls keep rushing towards me and I keep pushing them away.' He said, 'How can I help?' I said, 'Break my arms!'

A suspicious-looking man is stopped at border control while driving a motorbike with a bag on the back. The customs official at the border crossing asks the man to produce his identification, which he does, and it all checks out fine. He then asks, 'What's in the bag?' The man on the bike replies, 'Sand.' Lo and behold, when the bag is checked, it just contains sand. Having remembered the odd case of the man on a motorbike with a bag of sand, the guy at customs recognises the same suspicious man coming to the same border crossing twice a month for six months, always with a bag of sand, and always with the right identification. After those six months, curiosity gets the better of the customs official, and the next time he sees the man on the bike he stops him for a chat. 'Listen, mate,' he says. 'You've been coming here every two weeks for six months, always with a bag of sand that checks out. I can never find anything on you, but I'm convinced you are smuggling something across the border. If you tell me how you are getting away with it, I promise I won't arrest you. I'm just curious.' The man gives him a long stare, but eventually says slowly, 'Are you sure you won't arrest me?' The custom official swears to God that he will not tell a soul, and it's only to stop him wondering about it. 'Fine,' the man says. 'I *have* been smuggling something over the border.' 'What is it?!' cries the customs official. The man replies, 'Motorcycles.'

Why did the chicken cross the road? To escape North Korea's long-range missiles.

People tell me that I have a unique way of lighting up a room. It's called arson and those people are called witnesses.

I've always wondered what women got up to in the ladies' toilets when they all disappear together on a night out, but now I know. They take pictures of each other to post on Facebook.

Little Johnny was playing with something in the road, and his local vicar came up to him and said, 'Hello, little Johnny, what are you playing with?' Little Johnny said, 'sulphuric acid.' The vicar said, 'You mustn't play with that, it's dangerous.' Little Johnny said, 'I don't tell you not to play with holy water.' The vicar said, 'No, because holy water is good ... The other day I put holy water on a pregnant woman's tummy and she passed a baby boy.' 'That's nothing,' Little Johnny said. 'The other day I put sulphuric acid on my dog's bollocks and he passed a Ferrari.'

A friend of mine went to a shrink and said, 'Doctor, my wife is unfaithful to me. Every evening, she goes to Larry's bar and picks up men. In fact, she sleeps with anybody who asks her! I'm going crazy. What do you think I should do?' 'Relax,' says the doctor, 'take a deep breath and calm down. Now, tell me, exactly where is Larry's bar?'

As the coffin is being lowered into the ground at a traffic warden's funeral, a voice from inside shouts, 'I'm not dead, I'm not dead! Let me out!' The vicar smiles, leans forward sucking air through his teeth and mutters, 'Too late, pal, paperwork's already done.'

The mother of a seventeen-year-old girl was concerned that her daughter was having sex. Worried the girl might become pregnant and bring shame on the family, she consulted the family doctor. The doctor told her that teenagers today were very wilful and any attempt to stop the girl would probably result in rebellion. He then told her to arrange for her daughter to be put on birth control and until then, talk to her and give her a box of condoms. Later that evening, as her daughter was preparing for a date, the mother told her about the situation and handed her a box of condoms. The girl burst out laughing and reached over to hug her mother, saying, 'Oh, Mum! You don't have to worry about that! I'm dating Susan!'

A teenage boy had just passed his driving test and enquired of his father as to when they could discuss his use of the car. His father said he'd make a deal with his son: 'You bring your grades up from a C to a B average, study your Bible a little, and get your hair cut. Then we'll talk about the car.' The boy thought about that for a moment, decided he'd settle for the offer, and they agreed on it. After about six weeks, his father said, 'Son, you've brought your grades up and I've observed that you have been studying your Bible, but I'm disappointed you haven't had your hair cut.' The boy said, 'You know, Dad, I've been thinking about that, and I've noticed in my studies of the Bible that Samson had long hair, John the Baptist had long hair, Moses had long hair … and there's even strong evidence that Jesus had long hair.' Dad replied: 'Did you also notice they all walked everywhere they went?'

I was visiting my daughter and son-in-law the other night when I asked if I could borrow a newspaper. 'This is the twenty-first century, old man,' he said. 'We don't waste money on newspapers. Here, you can borrow my iPad.' I can tell you, that bloody fly never knew what hit it.

A business owner was confused about an invoice, so he called his secretary in to help. 'You graduated from university. If I were to give you £20,000, minus 14 per cent, how much would you take off?' The secretary thought a moment, and replied, 'Everything but my earrings.'

A dentist pulls out a numbing needle to give a man an injection. 'No way! No needles. I hate needles,' the patient said. The dentist starts to hook up the nitrous oxide and the man says, 'I can't do the gas thing. The thought of having the gas mask on suffocates me!' The dentist then asks the patient if he has any objections to taking a pill. 'No objection,' he says. 'I'm fine with pills.' The dentist gives him a couple of pills. He swallows them. 'What are they?' he says. 'Viagra,' says the dentist. 'Heck,' the patient says, 'I didn't know Viagra worked as a painkiller.' 'It doesn't,' says the dentist, 'But it will give you something to hold on to when I pull out your tooth.'

It was mealtime during an airline flight. 'Would you like dinner?' the flight attendant asked John, seated in front. 'What are my choices?' John asked. 'Yes or no,' she replied.

A flight attendant was stationed at the departure gate to check tickets. As a man approached, she extended her hand for the ticket and he opened his trench coat and flashed her. Without missing a beat, she said, 'Sir, I need to see your ticket, not your stub.'

A lady was picking through the frozen turkeys at the grocery store but she couldn't find one big enough for her family. She asked a stock boy, 'Do these turkeys get any bigger?' The stock boy replied, 'No, ma'am, they're dead.'

The police officer got out of his car as the kid who was stopped for speeding rolled down his window. 'I've been waiting for you all day,' the officer said. The kid replied, 'Yeah, well, I got here as fast as I could.' When the cop finally stopped laughing, he sent the kid on his way without a ticket.

A truck driver was driving along on the freeway and noticed a sign that read 'Low Bridge Ahead'. Before he knows it, the bridge is right in front of him and his truck gets wedged under it. Cars are backed up for miles. Finally a police car comes up. The officer gets out of his car and walks to the truck driver, puts his hands on his hips and says, 'Got stuck, huh?' The truck driver says, 'No, I was delivering this bridge and I ran out of gas.'

A college teacher reminds her class of tomorrow's final exam. 'Now class, I won't tolerate any excuses for you not being here tomorrow. I might consider a nuclear attack or a serious personal injury, illness, or a death in your immediate family, but that's it, no other excuses whatsoever!' A smart-ass student in the back of the room raised his hand and asked, 'What would you say if tomorrow I said I was suffering from complete and utter sexual exhaustion?' The entire class is reduced to laughter and snickering. When silence was restored, the teacher smiled knowingly at the student, shook her head and sweetly said, 'Well, I guess you'd have to write the exam with your other hand.'

A woman is standing nude looking in the bedroom mirror. She is not happy with what she sees and says to her husband, 'I feel horrible; I look old, fat and ugly. I really need you to pay me a compliment.' The husband replies, 'Your eyesight's damn near perfect.'

A man with a winking problem is applying for a job as a sales rep for a large firm. He has the best education, reputation and experience. The HR officer said, 'Normally, we'd hire you in a heartbeat, but sales is a highly visible occupation and your constant winking problem might upset customers. I'm sorry but we can't hire you.' 'But wait,' said the man. 'If I take two aspirin, my winking stops. Here, let me show you.' So he reached into his pockets for aspirin, and different packages of condoms fell out all over the desk and floor. Finally he found the aspirin, took two, and stopped winking. 'That's amazing,' said the HR officer. 'However, this is a reputable company and we can't hire someone who is into womanising as much as you appear to be.' Astounded, the man said, 'Womanising? What do you mean? I'm a happily married man!' 'Well then,' asked the HR officer, 'How do you explain all these condoms?' 'Oh, that,' he sighed. 'Have you ever walked into a pharmacy winking and asked for aspirin?'

A guy goes to the supermarket and notices a very attractive woman waving at him. She says, 'Hello.' He's rather taken aback, because he can't place her. So he asks, 'Do you know me?' To which she replies, 'I think that you're the father of one of my kids.' His mind races back to the only time he has ever been unfaithful to his wife. He asks, 'Are you the stripper at the stag party I made love to on the pool table, while all of my buddies were watching?' She looks into his eyes and says calmly, 'No, I'm your son's teacher.'

A man lies on his deathbed, surrounded by his family: a weeping wife and four children. Three of the children are tall, good looking and athletic, but the fourth and youngest is an ugly runt. 'Darling wife,' the husband whispers, 'assure me that the youngest child really is mine. I want to know the truth before I die, I will forgive you if…' The wife gently interrupts him. 'Yes, my dearest, absolutely, no question, I swear on my mother's grave that you are his father.' The man then dies, happy. The wife mutters under her breath, 'Thank God he didn't ask about the other three.'

A young boy enters a barber shop and the barber whispers to his customer, 'This is the dumbest kid in the world. Watch while I prove it to you.' The barber puts a five-pound note in one hand and a 50p coin in the other, then calls the boy over and asks, 'Which do you want, son?' The boy takes the 50p and leaves. 'What did I tell you?' said the barber. 'That kid never learns!' Later, when the customer leaves, he sees the same young boy coming out of the ice-cream store. 'Hey, son! May I ask you a question? Why did you take the change instead of the note?' The boy licked his cone and replied, 'Because the day I take the fiver, the game is over!'

Three guys, stranded on a desert island, find a magic lantern containing a genie, who grants them each one wish. The first guy wishes he was off the island and back home. The second guy wishes the same. The third guy says, 'I'm lonely. I wish my friends were back here.'

A newlywed couple moves into their new house. One day the husband comes home from work and his wife says, 'Honey, you know, in the upstairs bathroom one of the pipes is leaking, could you fix it?' The husband says, 'What do I look like, Mr Plumber?' A few days go by, and he comes home from work and his wife says, 'Honey, my tyre is flat. Could you change it for me?' He says, 'What do I look like, Mr Michelin?' Another few days go by, and it's raining pretty hard. The wife finds a leak in the roof. She says, 'Honey, there's a leak on the roof! Can you please fix it?' He says, 'What do I look like, Bob Vila?' The next day the husband comes home, and the roof is fixed. So is the plumbing. So is the car. He asks his wife what happened. 'Oh, I had a handyman come in and fix them,' she says. 'Great! How much is that going to cost me?' he snarls. Wife says, 'Nothing. He said he'd do it for free if I either baked him a cake or slept with him.' 'Uh, well, what kind of cake did you make?' asks the husband. 'What do I look like,' she says, 'Betty Crocker?'

A salesman goes up to a house and knocks on the front door. It is opened by a ten-year-old boy who has a lit cigar in one hand, a glass of whisky in the other and a porno mag tucked under his arm. The salesman asks,

'Hello son. Is your mum or dad home?' The little boy says, 'What do you think?'

Two little kids are in a hospital, lying on stretchers next to each other outside the operating room, the first surgeries of the day. The first kid leans over and asks, 'What are you in here for?' The second kid says, 'I'm getting my tonsils out, and I'm afraid'. The first kid says, 'You've got nothing to worry about. I had that done when I was four. They put you to sleep, and when you wake up they give you lots of jelly and ice cream. It's a breeze.' The second kid then asks, 'What are you here for?' The first kid says, 'Circumcision.' 'Whoa!' the second kid replies. 'Good luck, buddy. I had that done when I was born. Couldn't walk for a year.'

I was on a plane and we were coming in to land, and it affects your ears, doesn't it? So the stewardess gave me chewing gum. I put it in my ear. Took two days to get it out.

I got stopped last night by a policeman. He said, 'I'd like to follow you to the nearest police station.' I said, 'What for?' He said, 'I've forgotten the way.'

A man walks into a greengrocer's and says, 'I want five pounds of potatoes, please.' And the greengrocer says, 'We only sell kilos.' So the man says, 'All right then, I'll have five pounds of kilos.'

I knocked at my friend's door and his wife answered. I said, 'Is Jim in?' She didn't reply, just stood there looking at me. So I asked again. Just then a woman appeared at his wife's elbow. 'Sorry, love,' she said. 'We buried him last Thursday.' 'He didn't say anything about a pot of yellow paint before he went, did he?'

I went to Millets and said, 'I want to buy a tent.' A shop assistant said, 'To camp?' I said in a deep voice, 'Sorry, I want to buy a tent. And I also want to buy a caravan.' She said, 'Camper?' I replied in my most flamboyant manner, 'Make your mind up.'

A man walks into a doctor's office. 'What seems to be the problem?' asks the doc. 'It's ... um ... well ... I have five penises,' replies the man. 'Blimey!' says the doctor, 'How do your trousers fit?' 'Like a glove.'

A man goes to a fancy-dress party dressed only in his Y-fronts. A woman comes up to him and says, 'What are you supposed to be?' The man says, 'A premature ejaculation.' 'What?' asks the woman. The man explains, 'I've just come in my pants.'

A tribe of South American Indians living in voluntary isolation near Peru's south-eastern Amazon region has made a tense attempt to contact the outside world for a second time. After hours of work, it turns out their message said, 'Please tell the bastard, no more Candy Crush requests.'

I have a friend who is a Jehovah's Witness. He tried to tell me a knock-knock joke and got all pissed off when I ignored him.

I didn't get the IT job as apparently I'm not 'tech savvy'. I'm so annoyed, I'm getting my friend to send them an angry fax email thingy.

My boss phoned me at eight o'clock on Saturday morning. 'Accounts just called,' he said. 'Can you work all weekend?' 'I told you yesterday, I'm doing my garden,' I replied. 'I've got a bonfire started, and the shredder's set up as well.' 'That's a relief,' he replied. 'We'll be over in half an hour, the auditors are here on Monday.'

Grandma asked her grandsons, 'Do you want to go to the shops with me?' They ummed and ahhed and their father suggested that they should go, as she was leaving the next day and they'd miss her when she was gone. 'OK then. Are you coming too, Dad?' 'Christ no.'

A man calls the hospital and in a panic he says, 'Hello, I think my wife is going into labour, what should I do?' 'Calm down,' says the receptionist. 'Is this her first child?' 'No, it's her husband, you daft bint!'

I went to a fortune teller last week. She studied my hand and said, 'You have been masturbating.' I said, 'Hey, you are good. Can you tell me anything about my future?' She looked at my face and said, 'You'll be doing it for a fucking long time.'

Simon goes on *Stars in their Eyes*, Mathew Kelly notices he's in a wheelchair and asks, 'What happened?' Simon replies, 'I was in a car crash with my uncle, he died, and I had my legs amputated, but they saved my uncle's legs and grafted them onto me. In six months' time I will be able to walk again.' 'That's amazing,' says Matthew. 'And who are you going to be tonight?' Simon says, 'Tonight, Matthew, I'm going to be Simon and Half Uncle.'

Three men die on Christmas Eve. To get into heaven, St Peter says, 'you must have something on you that represents Christmas.' The Englishman flicks on his lighter and says it's a candle. St Peter lets him pass. The Welshman pulls out a set of keys, jingles them and says they are bells. St Peter lets him pass. The Irishman pulls out his ten-inch penis and St Peter says, 'How does that represent Christmas?' Paddy says, 'It's a cracker isn't it!'

Paddy wants to become a priest, so he goes to see the bishop, who says, 'First you must answer three questions on the Bible. First, who was born in a stable?' 'Red Rum,' replies Paddy. 'Second, do you know anything about Damascus?' 'It kills 99 per cent of all known germs,' says Paddy. 'Third, what happened when the disciples went to Mount Olive?' 'Don't know that one. Did Popeye kick the shit out of them?'

The wife asked me what I was doing on the computer last night. I told her I was looking for cheap flights. 'I love you!' she said, then she got all excited, unzipped my trousers and gave me the most amazing blow job ever ... which is odd because she's never shown an interest in darts before.

An Englishman, a Frenchman, a Spaniard and a German are walking down the street together. A juggler is performing on the street but there are so many people that the four men can't see him. So the juggler goes on top of a platform and asks, 'Can you see me now?' The four men answer, 'Yes.' 'Oui.' 'Si.' 'Ja.'

An infinite number of mathematicians walk into a bar. The bartender says, 'What'll it be, boys?' The first mathematician: 'I'll have one half of a beer.' The second mathematician: 'I'll have one quarter of a beer.' The third mathematician: 'I'll have one eighth of a beer.' The fourth mathematician: 'I'll have one sixteenth of a...' The bartender interrupts: 'Know your limits, boys,' as he pours out a single beer.

What does the 'B' in Benoit B. Mandelbrot stand for? Answer: Benoit B. Mandelbrot.

Jean-Paul Sartre is sitting at a French café, revising his draft of *Being and Nothingness*. He says to the waitress, 'I'd like a cup of coffee, please, with no cream.' The waitress replies, 'I'm sorry, Monsieur, but we're out of cream. How about with no milk?'

A classics professor goes to a tailor to get his trousers mended. The tailor asks, 'Euripides?' The professor replies, 'Yes. Eumenides?'

A programmer's wife tells him, 'Go to the shop and pick up a loaf of bread. If they have eggs, get a dozen.' The programmer comes home with twelve loaves of bread.

Two dwarfs go to a brothel. They both pick their women and proceed to the bedrooms. Dwarf no. 1 cannot get it up; no matter how hard he tries, he's as limp as can be. Despondent, he goes to sleep pondering his missed opportunity. Before he falls asleep, he can hear the second dwarf through the walls... 'One, two, three ... one, two, three ... one, two, three ... one, two, three...' The next morning they meet up and discuss the previous night's events. The second dwarf asks the first how he got on, 'Oh, I just couldn't get it up, no matter how hard I tried. What about you though?' he says. 'You sounded like you were having fun?' 'Me? I couldn't even get on the bed!'

Paddy and his wife were discussing their sex life. Paddy said, 'I want to try that wheelbarrow position tonight.' His wife asked, 'What is that?' Paddy told her, 'You bend over, put your hands on the floor, then I pick your legs up and take you from behind!' His wife said, 'Hmm, OK, I'll do it on two conditions. First, if it hurts you stop immediately, and second ... we don't go past my mother's house!'

Jesus and Moses are avid golfers, and every chance they get they will visit the great greens worldwide. This one day they were playing golf on one of their favourite greens, enjoying the day off and relaxing with a day of golf. As they walked up over the hill they came across an elderly gentleman. They teamed up and began to play. At the next hole, Jesus stepped up to the tee, carefully placed his ball, swung, and hit the ball. But the ball sliced and went into the water. Jesus walked over to the pond and then stepped out onto the water. That's right, not into the water but onto the water. He walked around on the water until he saw his ball. When he did, he held out his hand and the ball floated to the surface. From there, he played through and knocked the ball into the cup. He did a little victory dance right there on the water and then crossed to the other side. Moses grinned and stepped up to the tee himself. He swung and hit his ball. His ball also went into the water. He nodded at the older gentleman and walked over to the pond. There he put his golf club in his right hand. As he held his hands up over his head, the water parted, creating a path of dry land to the ball. From there, he hit the ball and the ball went into the cup. Then he walked out of the pond and the water closed behind him. The elderly gentleman solemnly stepped up to his tee and eyed the lane ahead of him. He measured the distance, noted the wind direction and looked over at the hole. At last, he swung. The ball flew up, arched, and then landed in the centre of the pond. When it hit the water, a fish swallowed it. As the fish was swimming, a hawk swooped down from the sky and snatched up the fish. As the bird was flying, a bolt of lightning suddenly flashed in the path of the bird and it dropped the fish. The fish fell onto the back of a turtle that was walking up the green. When the fish hit the turtle, the ball rolled out of its mouth and started to roll away from the hole. But as it was rolling a squirrel picked it up mistaking it for a nut. As the squirrel ran toward a tree a rabbit ran across its path. This frightened the squirrel and it dropped the ball, which rolled down the green and into the cup – a hole in one! Jesus and Moses both looked at the elderly gentleman. 'Come on, Dad,' Jesus sighed. 'Are you going to mess around or play golf?'

A man walks into a bar with a steering wheel shoved down his pants. The barman looks at him curiously and says, 'Buddy, you know you got a steering wheel shoved down your pants?' The man answers, 'Yeah, I know! It's been driving me nuts all day.'

My fake plants died because I didn't pretend to water them.

Guy walks into a bar and sits at a table. Tells the waitress, 'I'll have a Bloody Mary and a menu.' When she returns with his drink, he asks, 'Still serving breakfast?' When she says yes, he replies, 'Then I'll have two eggs – runny on top and burnt on the bottom – five strips of bacon – well done on one end and still raw on the other – two pieces of burnt toast and a cold cup of coffee.' Indignantly, the waitress says, 'We don't serve that kind of stuff in here!' Guy says, 'Funny … that's what I had in here yesterday…'

A panda walks into a bar and orders a beer and a hamburger. After he eats he stands up stretches and pulls out a gun, shooting everyone in the room but the bartender. The panda puts £20 on the bar and turns to leave. As he walks out the door the bartender asks why he shot everyone. The panda tells him to look in the encyclopaedia. The bartender looks up 'panda' and reads, 'Panda: Large black and white mammal native to China. Eats shoots and leaves.'

A guy walks into a bar and asks for ten shots of the establishment's finest single malt scotch. The bartender sets them up, and the guy takes the first shot in the row and pours it on the floor. He then takes the last one in the row and does the same. The bartender asks him, 'Why did you do that?' And the guy replies, 'Well, the first shot always tastes like crap, and the last one always makes me sick.'

A priest, a rabbi, and a pastor are sitting in a bar, across the street from a brothel. They are sipping their drinks when they see a rabbi walk in to the brothel. 'Oy! It's awful to see a man of the cloth give into temptation,' says the rabbi. A short while later, they see a pastor walk into the brothel. 'Damn! It's terrible to see a man of the cloth give into such temptation,' says the pastor. In a little bit, they see a priest enter the brothel. 'It's nice to see the ladies, who have been used so poorly, have time to confess their sins,' says the priest.

A guy walks into a bar. He asks the bartender, 'Do you have any helicopter-flavoured crisps?' The bartender shakes his head. 'No, we only have plain.'

A Scotsman, an Englishman and an Irishman are sitting in a bar in New York reminiscing about home. 'Back in me pub in Glasgow,' brags the Scotsman, 'fer every four pints of stout I order, they give me one fer free!' 'In me pub in London,' says the Englishman, 'I pay fer two pint's o' Guinness and they give me a third one free!' 'That's nothing,' says the Irishman, 'in my pub back in Dublin, you walk up to the bar, they give the first pint fer free, the second pint fer free, the third pint fer free – and then they take you upstairs and you have sex for FREE!' 'Is that true?' asks the Scotsman. 'Has that really happened to you?' 'Well, no,' says the Irishman, 'but it happens to me sister all the time!'

Horse walks into a bar. Bartender says, 'So, why the long face?'

Two guys are sitting in a bar. One guy says, 'I slept with my wife before we were married, did you?' The other guy says, 'I don't know – what was her maiden name?'

A woman and a duck walk into a bar. The bartender asks, 'Where'd you get the pig?' The woman says, 'That's not a pig, that's a duck.' He says, 'I was talking to the duck.'

So a guy walks into a bar, looking really moody, and immediately orders a double whisky. Then he starts rambling on about how lousy a wife he's got, until the bartender finally says: 'You know, I don't understand what you're complaining about. All the other guys in here only have compliments about your wife.'

A skunk walks into a bar and says, 'Hey where did everybody go?'

E-flat walks into a bar. The bartender says, 'Sorry, we don't serve minors.'

A potato walked into a bar. All eyes were on him.

A cowboy walked into a bar and ordered a whiskey. When the bartender delivered the drink, the cowboy asked, 'Where is everybody?' The bartender replied, 'They've gone to the hanging.' 'Hanging? Who are they hanging?' 'Brown Paper Pete,' the bartender replied. 'What kind of a name is that?' the cowboy asked. 'Well,' said the bartender, 'he wears a brown paper hat, brown paper shirt, brown paper trousers and brown paper shoes.' 'Weird guy,' said the cowboy. 'What are they hanging him for?' 'Rustling,' said the bartender.

Two guys are sitting at a bar. One guy says to the other, 'Do you know that lions have sex ten or fifteen times a night?' The other guy says, 'Damn, I just joined the Rotary Club.'

A termite walks into a bar and says, 'Is the bartender here?'

A guy walks into a bar. There's nobody there except the bartender and a beautiful woman, sitting at the other end of the bar. The man says, 'I'm buying that woman a drink.' The bartender says, 'You don't want to do that. She's a lesbian.' The man says, 'I don't care, give her the drink.' After the woman gets the drink, she raises the glass to her benefactor. The man strolls over to her. He says, 'Hi. I'm Bill Williams from Terre Haute. So how are things in Beirut?'

What do you call a Bohemian that gets thrown out of a bar? A bounced Czech.

Fist Bump. The most extreme book in the Mr Men series.

What's the difference between a 16-inch pizza and a jazz musician? A 16-inch pizza can feed a family of four.

A duck walks into a bar and says to the bartender, 'I'd like to buy some peanuts.' The bartender says, 'Sorry, we don't sell peanuts.' The duck leaves. Next day, the duck walks into the bar and says, 'I want to buy some peanuts.' The bartender replies, 'I already told you, I don't sell peanuts!' The duck leaves. Next day, the duck walks into the bar and says, 'I want to buy some peanuts.' The bartender yells back, 'I told you, I don't sell peanuts! If you ask one more time, I'll nail you to the wall!' So the duck leaves. Next day, the duck walks into the bar and says, 'Do you have any nails?' The bartender says,

'Sorry, we don't have nails.' The duck asks, 'Do you have any peanuts?'

A guy walks into a bar with his pet monkey. He orders a drink and while he's drinking, the monkey jumps all around the place. The monkey grabs some olives off the bar and eats them. Then he grabs some sliced limes and eats them. He then jumps onto the pool table and grabs one of the billiard balls. To everyone's amazement, he sticks it in his mouth and somehow swallows it whole. The bartender screams at the guy, 'Did you see what your monkey just did?' 'No, what?' 'He just ate the cue ball off my pool table – whole!' 'Yeah, that doesn't surprise me,' replied the guy. 'He eats everything in sight. Sorry! I'll pay for the cue ball and stuff.' The guy finishes his drink, pays his bill, pays for the stuff the monkey ate and leaves. Two weeks later the guy is in the bar again, and has his monkey with him. He orders a drink and the monkey starts running around the bar again. While the man is finishing his drink, the monkey finds a maraschino cherry on the bar. He grabs it, sticks it up his butt, pulls it out, and eats it. Then the monkey finds a peanut, and again sticks it up his butt, pulls it out, and eats it. The bartender is disgusted. 'Did you see what your monkey did just now?' 'No, what?' replied the man. 'Well, he stuck both a maraschino cherry and a peanut up his butt, pulled them out, and ate them!' said the bartender. 'Yeah, that doesn't surprise me,' replied the guy. 'He still eats everything in sight, but ever since he had to shit that cue ball out, he measures everything first now.'

So a guy walks into a bar after a round of golf and sits down at a table opposite a flashily dressed blonde who says to him, 'I'm a hooker.' He says, 'Well, if you turn your hands on the shaft a little bit to the left … you'll tend more towards a slice.'

A non-renewable natural resource walks in to a bar and orders a tall glass of whiskey. The bartender says, 'Sorry, friend, I can't serve you. You've been getting wasted all day long.'

Thomas Edison walks into a bar and orders a beer. The bartender says, 'OK, I'll serve you a beer, just don't get any ideas.'

A guy walks into a bar and sees a horse tending the bar, apron and all, wiping out a glass. He stares at the horse for a minute without saying a word. The horse returns the stare and breaks the silence by asking, 'Hey buddy, what's the matter? You can't believe that a horse can tend bar?' 'No,' the guy says, 'I can't believe that the ferret sold the place.'

An Irishman walks into a bar and tells the bartender, 'I'll have three rounds, all at once.' So the bartender gets his order but says to the man, 'Sir, you'd enjoy them better if I served them to you one at a time.' The Irishman replies, 'No, it's a tradition. Back in Dublin, my brothers and I would all go to the pub and have a round together. I moved over here a few years ago but I still keep the tradition.' Touched by the story, the bartender serves the rounds, and goes about his business. The Irishman returns for several nights. One night, the Irishman comes in and only orders two rounds. The bartender, shaken, asks, 'What happened? Did one of your brothers die?' The Irishman laughs and replies, 'No, I quit drinking!'

A guy walks into a bar and sits down. He orders a beer, and another, and another, and so on, until finally the bartender asks him to leave. He walks out the side door, and a few seconds later, he walks in the front door, sits down, orders a drink, and the bartender asks him to leave. He gets up, walks out the side door, and comes back in the front door and is asked to leave. This happens about eight more times, until on the ninth, the man exclaims, 'How many bars do you work in, man?'

Two guys are walking their dogs, a black lab and a Chihuahua. Passing a bar, the labrador walker says, 'Let's get a beer.' The other replies, 'We can't take our dogs in there.' The first says, 'Watch.' In he goes and orders a beer. 'Sorry, you can't bring your dog in here.' 'He's my seeing-eye dog.' 'Oh. Sorry. Here's your beer.' The other guy follows, orders a beer. Same response: 'No dogs allowed.' 'He's my seeing-eye dog.' 'Yeah, right. A Chihuahua? Give me a break.' 'They gave me a CHIHUAHUA?!'

An amnesiac walks into a bar. The bartender asks, 'What can I get you today?' The amnesiac says, 'I don't know, I have trouble remembering things.' The bartender says, 'Like what?'

A guy walks into a bar. The bartender asks, 'How's it going?' 'OK, I guess. Holding my own.' 'That's good.' replies the bartender. 'You'd get arrested if you held someone else's.'

Julius Caesar walks into a bar. 'I'll have a martinus,' he says. The bartender gives him a puzzled look and asks, 'Don't you mean a "martini"?' 'Look,' Caesar retorts, 'If I wanted a double, I'd have asked for it.'

So Jesus walks into a bar and says, 'I'll just have a glass of water.'

A dyslexic walks into a bra.

A guy walks into a barber shop and asks, 'Bob Peters here?' The barber replies, 'Nope. Just cut hair.'

A guy walks into a wedding reception. He goes up to the bartender and asks, 'Is this the punch line?'

A guy walks into a bar after a long day at work and orders a drink. After his first sip, he hears a high-pitched voice. 'Hey, mister! Nice pants!' it says. He looks around, doesn't see anything, and quickly shrugs it off. After a little bit, he takes another sip and hears the voice again. 'Hey, mister! Sweet shoes!' Again, he looks around, sees nothing but a bartender who is busy attending to other customers. Shaking his head, he sips once more. 'Hey mister! Cool shirt!' He puts down his drink, frustrated at this phantom voice, and signals to the bartender, who comes over. 'Hey, barkeep,' he begins, 'what is that high-pitched voice I keep hearing?' 'Oh, those are the peanuts,' he replies. 'They're complimentary.'

This guy walks into a bar and says to the bartender, 'If I can show you something unbelievable, will you give me a free beer?' The bartender says, 'All right.' So the man puts a hamster and two frogs on the bar and all of a sudden the two frogs jump up and launch into a Broadway medley. Well, a man at the end of the bar said, 'That's amazing, I'll give you $1,000 for the frogs.' The man agreed, and the guy took off. The bartender said to him, 'You could have gotten more for the frogs.' The man said, 'Frogs are easy to come by, the hamster's a ventriloquist.'

Guy walks into a bar and pulls a tiny grand piano out of his pocket. Then he pulls out a little guy who sits down and begins to play. 'Where'd ya get that?' the bartender asks. 'I have a magic bottle – you rub it and get a wish,' the customer replies. The customer agrees to let the bartender try it, and pulls a dirty old whisky bottle from his pocket. The bartender rubs it, and the room fills up with ducks, flying everywhere. 'I didn't wish for a million "ducks",' says bartender. 'No,' replies the customer. 'Do you think I wished for a ten-inch pianist?'

Three guys are drinking in a bar when a drunk comes in, staggers up to them, and points at the guy in the middle, shouting, 'Your mum's the best sex in town!' Everyone expects a fight, but the guy ignores him, so the drunk wanders off and bellies up to the bar at the far end. Ten minutes later, the drunk comes back, points at the same guy, and says, 'I just did your mum, and it was sw-e-et!' Again, the guy refuses to take the bait, and the drunk goes back to the far end of the bar. Ten minutes later, he comes back and announces, 'Your mum liked it!' Finally, the guy interrupts. 'Go home, Dad, you're drunk.'

An Irishman walks by a bar … it could happen.

Ole goes to a bar to meet his friend, Sven. He spies Sven sitting at the bar, with a dog underneath his chair. Ole says, 'Hey, Sven, does your dog bite?' 'No, Ole,' says Sven, 'he don't.' 'Well, can I pet the dog?' 'Sure,' says Sven. Ole reaches down to pet the dog, and the dog bites him on the hand. 'Hey,' says Ole, 'I thought you said your dog doesn't bite?' 'Oh,' says Ole, 'that ain't my dog.'

A baby seal walks into a bar, and the bartender says, 'What will it be, stranger?' The seal replies, 'I'll have anything as long it's not a Canadian Club.'

A guy walks into a bar and yells, 'All lawyers are assholes.' The man at the end of the bar says, 'I object to that remark'. The guy asks, 'Why, are you a lawyer?' The man says, 'No, I'm an asshole.'

A little guy is sitting at the bar just staring at his drink for half an hour when this big trouble-making biker steps up next to him, grabs his drink and gulps it down in one swig. The poor little guy starts crying. 'Come on, man. I was just giving you a hard time,' the biker says. 'I didn't think you'd *cry*.' 'I can't stand to see a man crying.' 'This is the worst day of my life,' says the little guy between sobs. 'I can't do anything right.' 'I overslept and was late to an important meeting, so my boss fired me. When I went to the parking lot, I found my car was stolen and I don't have any insurance. I left my wallet in the cab I took home. I found my wife in bed with the gardener, and my dog bit me. So I came to this bar trying to work up the courage to put an end to my life, and then you show up and drink the damn poison.'

Two Texas farmers, Jim and Bob, are sitting at their favourite bar, drinking beer. Jim turns to Bob and says, 'You know, I'm tired of going through life without an education. Tomorrow I think I'll go to the community college and sign up for some classes.' Bob thinks it's a good idea, and the two leave. The next day, Jim goes down to the college and meets the dean of admissions, who signs him up for the four basic classes: maths, English, history and logic. 'Logic?' Jim says. 'What's that?' The dean says, 'I'll give you an example. Do you own a weed eater?' 'Yeah.' 'Then logically speaking, because you own a weed eater, I think that you would have a yard.' 'That's true, I do have a yard!' 'I'm not done,' the dean says. 'Because you have a yard, I think logically that you would have a house.' 'Yes, I do have a house.' 'And because you have a house, I think that you might logically have a family.' 'That's true, I do have a family!' 'I'm not done yet. Because you have a family, then logically you must have a wife. And because you have a wife, then logic tells me you must be a heterosexual.' 'I am a heterosexual! That's amazing; you were able to find out all of that because I have a weed eater.' Excited to take the class now, Jim shakes the dean's hand and leaves to go meet Bob at the bar. He tells Bob about his classes and how he is signed up for maths, English, history and logic. 'Logic?' Bob says, 'What's that?' Jim says, 'I'll give you an example. Do you have a weed eater?' 'No.' 'Then you're a queer.'

A drunk walks into a bar. 'Ouch!' he says.

A skeleton walks into a bar and says, 'Give me a beer and a mop.'

So a guy walks into a bar with a pair of jumper cables around his neck. The bartender looks at him and says gruffly, 'All right, pal, I'll let you stay but don't start anything.'

A married Irishman went into the confessional and said to his priest, 'I almost had an affair with another woman.' The priest said, 'What do you mean, almost?' The Irishman said, 'Well, we got undressed and rubbed together, but then I stopped.' The priest said, 'Rubbing together is the same as putting it in. You're not to see that woman again. For your penance, say five Hail Marys and put £50 in the poor box.' The Irishman left the confessional, said his prayers, and then walked over to the poor box. He paused for a moment and then started to leave. The priest, who was watching, quickly ran over to him saying, 'I saw that. You didn't put any money in the poor box!' The Irishman replied, 'Yeah, but I rubbed the £50 on the box, and according to you, that's the same as putting it in.'

There once was a religious young woman who went to confession. Upon entering the confessional she said, 'Forgive me, Father, for I have sinned.' The priest said, 'Confess your sins and be forgiven.' The young woman said, 'Last night my boyfriend made mad passionate love to me seven times.' The priest thought long and hard and then said, 'Squeeze seven lemons into a glass and then drink the juice.' The young woman asked, 'Will this cleanse me of my sins?' The priest said, 'No, but it will wipe that smile off your face.'

Muldoon lived alone in the Irish countryside with only a pet dog for company. One day the dog died, and Muldoon went to the parish priest and asked, 'Father, my dog is dead. Could you be saying a Mass for the poor creature?' Father Patrick replied, 'I'm afraid not; we cannot have services for an animal in the church. But there are some Baptists down the lane, and there's no telling what they believe. Maybe they'll do something for the creature.' Muldoon said, 'I'll go right away Father. Do you think £5,000 is enough to donate to them for the service?' Father Patrick exclaimed, 'Sweet Mary, Mother of Jesus! Why didn't you tell me the dog was Catholic?'

A man goes to heaven and St Peter shows him around. They go past one room and the man asks, 'Who are all those people in there?' 'They are the Methodists,' says St Peter. They pass another room and the man asks the same question. 'They are the Anglicans,' says St Peter. As they're approaching the next room St Peter says, 'Take your shoes off and tip-toe by as quietly as you can.' 'Why, who's in there?' asks the man. 'The Catholics,' replies St Peter, 'and they think they're the only ones up here.'

Now, it seems there was this English soldier who went to Ireland for a holiday because he knew he could get the best whiskey there. Well, after having had quite a night of drinking he found himself wandering along the side of an Irish road at a very early hour of the morning. Coming up the road was an Irish farmer on his way to market. In his wagon was his prize pig and pulling the load was his best horse. When the Irishman saw the soldier he thought, 'Poor soldier. Out this early in the morning walking alone. I should offer him a ride.' So he pulled up next to the soldier and asked if he wanted a ride into town. Now the English soldier wasn't too sure about accepting a ride from an Irishman, especially when he saw, sitting on the floorboards, the farmer's rifle. But the farmer insisted and the soldier was quite drunk. When the soldier was in the wagon the farmer realised he was running late and coaxed his horse to go faster. Just at that moment a wild rabbit ran across the road and scared the horse. He broke into a mad gallop and no matter how hard the farmer tried to stop him, he would not slow down. Then, suddenly, the horse made a sharp turn and the wagon tipped over and everyone fell out. The soldier landed in a ditch, face down, and couldn't move. He knew he'd broken at least one arm and a leg. He was feeling dizzy and thought he might have sustained a concussion. He had trouble seeing from one eye and knew it was bleeding. From behind him he could hear the farmer moaning over what had happened. 'Oh, my poor pig! You've got a nasty cut in your side. I'd best be putting you out of your misery.' And the soldier heard the farmer fire his rifle into the pig. Then, the farmer saw his horse. 'Oh, my poor, poor horse! You've broken a leg. I'd best be putting you out of your misery.' And the soldier heard the farmer fire his rifle, again, into his horse. Then he heard the farmer coming closer to him. The farmer turned the soldier over and said, 'Oh, you poor soldier ... how are you?' The soldier said, quickly, 'I never felt better in my life!'

A drunk leaves a bar and decides to take a shortcut through a graveyard. It is raining heavily and very dark. The drunk fails to see an open grave and falls into it. He tries to climb out of it, but it is too deep and the rain has turned the dirt to mud and has made it too slippery to climb. He gives up after a while and decides to spend the night there. A while later, another drunk leaves the same bar and decides to take the same shortcut through the graveyard. He, too, falls into that open grave and tries to climb out but the mud is too slippery. The first drunk is still sitting there and watches as the other drunk tries but fails to get out. The first drunk stands up, taps the second drunk on the shoulder and tells him, 'You'll never get out!' He did.

Who says sticks and stones may break my bones, but words will never hurt me? Someone who's never been hit with a dictionary.

A rope walked into a restaurant and ordered a milkshake. The waiter said, 'Are you a rope?' The rope said, 'Yes.' The waiter said, 'We don't serve ropes.' So, the rope went out and burnt off his ends and tied himself into a knot. The rope went back into the restaurant and ordered a milkshake. The waiter asked, 'Are you a rope?' The rope said, 'No, I'm a frayed knot.'

How do you make a rock float? Put it in a glass with some ice cream and root beer.

A man went to church one day and afterwards he stopped to shake the vicar's hand. He said, 'Vicar, I'll tell you, that was a damned fine sermon. Damned good!' The vicar said, 'Thank you, sir, but I'd rather you didn't use profanity.' The man said, 'I was so damned impressed with that sermon, I put £5,000 in the offering plate!' The vicar said, 'No shit?'

A group of Britons were travelling by tour bus through Holland. As they stopped at a cheese farm, a young guide led them through the process of cheese making, explaining that goat's milk was used. She showed the group a lovely hillside where many goats were grazing. 'These', she explained, 'are the older goats put out to pasture when they no longer produce.' She then asked, 'What do you do in England with your old goats?' A spry old gentleman answered, 'They send us on bus tours!'

Brenda and Steve took their six-year-old son to the doctor. With some hesitation, they explained that although their little angel appeared to be in good health, they were concerned about his rather small penis. After examining the child, the doctor confidently declared, 'Just feed him pancakes. That should solve the problem.' The next morning when the boy arrived at breakfast, there was a large stack of warm pancakes in the middle of the table. 'Wow, Mum,' he exclaimed. 'Are these for me?' 'Just take two,' Brenda replied. 'The rest are for your father.'

Bob, a seventy-year-old, extremely wealthy widower, shows up at the country club with a breathtakingly beautiful 25-year-old blonde-haired woman who knocks everyone's socks off with her youthful sex appeal and charm and who hangs over Bob's arm and listens intently to his every word. His mates at the club are all aghast. At the very first chance, they corner him and ask, 'Bob, how'd you get the trophy girlfriend?' Bob replies, 'Girlfriend? She's my wife!' They are knocked over, but continue to ask. 'So, how'd you persuade her to marry you?' 'I lied about my age,' Bob replies. 'What, did you tell her you were only fifty?' Bob smiles and says, 'No, I told her I was ninety.'

A few years ago, Josef was finally given an exit permit by the Russians and allowed to immigrate to Israel to join his family. He was told that he could only take what he could pack into one suitcase. At Moscow Airport he was stopped by an enormous customs officer who glared at him and snarled, 'Open the case!' Josef opened the case and the Russian rummaged through the meagre belongings and pulled out a large bundle wrapped in old copies of *Pravda*. He unwrapped it to reveal a bust of Stalin. 'What is that?' snarled the customs officer. 'What is that?' said Josef timidly. 'You shouldn't ask "What is that?" You should ask "Who is that?" That is our glorious leader, Stalin. I'm taking it to my new home to remind me of all the wonderful things that he did and the marvellous life that I am leaving behind.' 'I always knew you Jews were mad!' said the official, tossing the bust into the case. 'Go!' A few hours later Josef arrived at Ben Gurion Airport and was confronted by an Israeli customs officer. 'Shalom. Welcome to Israel. Open the case!' Once again Josef's belongings were examined and the customs officer came upon the bust. 'What is that?' said the customs officer. 'What is that?' said Josef indignantly. 'You shouldn't ask "What is that?" You should ask "Who is that?" That is the bastard Stalin. I'm taking it to my new home to remind me of all the misery and suffering that he caused me for most of my life. I want to spit on it every day for the rest of my life.' 'I always knew you Russians were mad!' said the official, tossing the bust into the case. 'Go!' At last Josef arrived in his new home and eventually got around to unpacking, watched by his young nephew. He took out his few clothes and then carefully unwrapped the bust of Stalin and put it on a table. 'Who is that?' asked his nephew. 'Who is that?' said Josef with a smile. 'You shouldn't ask, "Who is that?" You should ask, "What is that?" That is five kilos of gold and a bit of black shoe polish!'

I saw a van with a bumper sticker saying 'I am a vet, therefore I drive like an animal.' Suddenly I realised how many gynaecologists there are on the roads.

Joe wants to buy a motorcycle. He doesn't have much luck, until one day he comes across a Harley with a 'for sale' sign on it. The bike looks better than a new one, although it is ten years old. It's shiny and in mint condition. He buys it and asks the seller how he kept it in such great condition for ten years. 'Well, it's quite simple,' says the seller. 'Whenever the bike is outside and it's gonna rain, rub Vaseline on the chrome. It protects it from the rain.' And he hands Joe a jar of Vaseline. That night, his girlfriend Susie invites him over to meet her parents. Naturally, they take the bike there. Just before they enter the house, Susie stops him and says, 'I have to tell you something about my family. When we eat dinner, we don't talk. In fact, the first person who says anything during dinner has to do the dishes.' 'No problem,' he says. And in they go. Joe is shocked. Right in the middle of the living room is a huge stack of dirty dishes. In the kitchen is another huge stack of dishes. Piled up on the stairs, in the corridor, everywhere he looks, dirty dishes. They sit down to dinner, and sure enough, no one says a word. As dinner progresses, Joe decides to take advantage of the situation. He leans over and kisses Susie. No one says a word. He reaches over and fondles her breasts. Nobody says a word. So he stands up, grabs her, throws her on the table and screws her, right there in front of her parents. His girlfriend is flustered, her dad is obviously livid and her mum of course completely horrified when he sits back down, but no one says a word. He looks at her mum. She's got a great body too. Joe grabs mum, bends her over the table and screws her every which way but loose right there on the dinner table. She has a big orgasm and Joe sits down. His girlfriend is furious, her dad is boiling and mum is beaming from ear to ear, but still … total silence. All of a sudden there is a loud clap of thunder, and it starts to rain. Joe remembers his bike, so he pulls the jar of Vaseline from his pocket. Suddenly the father shouts, 'OK, OK! I'LL DO THE DISHES!'

I was at the swimming baths yesterday and had a sneaky piss in the deep end. The lifeguard blew his whistle so loud, I nearly fell in.

It's the final of the World Cup, and a man makes his way to his seat right at pitchside. He sits down, noticing that the seat next to him is empty. He leans over and asks his neighbour if someone will be sitting there. 'No,' says the neighbour. 'The seat is empty.' 'This is incredible,' said the man. 'Who in their right mind would have a seat like this for the World Cup Final and not use it?' The neighbour says, 'Well, actually, the seat belongs to me. I was supposed to come with my wife, but she passed away. This is the first football game we haven't been to together since we got married.' 'Oh, I'm so sorry to hear that. That's terrible ... But couldn't you find someone else, a friend or relative, or even a neighbour to take the seat?' The man shakes his head. 'No,' he says. 'They're all at the funeral.'

Two campers are hiking in the woods when one is bitten on the rear end by a rattlesnake. 'I'll go into town for a doctor,' the other says. He runs ten miles to a small town and finds the town's only doctor, who is delivering a baby. 'I can't leave,' the doctor says. 'But here's what to do. Take a knife, cut a little X where the bite is, suck out the poison and spit it on the ground.' The guy runs back to his friend, who is in agony. 'What did the doctor say?' the victim asks. 'He says you're gonna die.'

Three kids come down to the kitchen and sit around the breakfast table. The mother asks the oldest boy what he'd like to eat. 'I'll have some fuckin' French toast,' he says. The mother is outraged at his language, hits him, and sends him upstairs. She asks the middle child what he wants. 'Well, I guess that leaves more fuckin' French toast for me,' he says. She is livid, smacks him, and sends him away. Finally she asks the youngest son what he wants for breakfast. 'I don't know,' he says meekly, 'but I definitely don't want the fuckin' French toast.'

A guy enters a bar carrying an alligator. He says to the patrons, 'Here's a deal. I'll open this alligator's mouth and place my genitals inside. The 'gator will close his mouth for one minute, then open it, and I'll remove my unit unscathed. If it works, everyone here buys me a drink.' The crowd agrees. The guy drops his pants and puts his privates in the alligator's mouth. The alligator closes its mouth. After a minute, the guy grabs a beer bottle and bangs the 'gator on the top of its head. The alligator opens wide, and he removes his genitals unscathed. Everyone buys him a drink. Then he says, 'I'll pay anyone who's willing to give it a try a hundred dollars.' After a while, a hand goes up in the back of the bar. It's a woman. 'I'll give it a try,' she says, 'but you have to promise not to hit me on the head with the beer bottle.'

On a passenger flight, the pilot comes over the public address system as usual to greet the passengers. He tells them at what altitude they'll be flying, the expected arrival time, and a bit about the weather, and advises them to relax and have a good flight. Then, forgetting to turn off the microphone, he says to his co-pilot, 'What would relax me right now is a cup of coffee and a blow job.' All the passengers hear it. As a stewardess immediately begins to run toward the cockpit to tell the pilot of his slip-up, one of the passengers stops her and says, 'Don't forget the coffee!'

A guy brings a dog to a talent scout. 'This dog can speak English,' he claims to the unimpressed agent. 'OK, sport,' the guy says to the dog, 'what's on the top of a house?' 'Roof!' the dog replies. 'Oh, come on,' the talent agent responds. 'All dogs go "roof".' 'No, wait,' the guy says. He asks the dog, 'What does sandpaper feel like?' 'Rough!' the dog answers. The talent agent gives a condescending blank stare. He is losing his patience. 'No, hang on,' the guy says. 'This one will amaze you.' He turns and asks the dog, 'Who, in your opinion, was the greatest baseball player of all time?' 'Ruth!' goes the dog. And the talent scout, having seen enough, boots them out of his office onto the street. And the dog turns to the guy and says, 'Maybe I should've gone for DiMaggio?'

Two campers are walking through the woods when a huge brown bear suddenly appears in the clearing about 50 feet in front of them. The bear sees the campers and begins to head towards them. The first guy drops his backpack, digs out a pair of running shoes, and frantically begins to put them on. The second guy says, 'What are you doing? Spikes won't help you outrun that bear.' 'I don't need to outrun the bear,' the first guy says. 'I just need to outrun you.'

A guy is sitting at home when he hears a knock at the door. He opens the door and sees a snail on the porch. He picks up the snail and throws it as far as he can. Three years later, there's a knock on the door. He opens it and sees the same snail. The snail says, 'What the hell was that all about?'

A man dies and is sent to Hell. Satan meets him, shows him doors to three rooms, and says he must choose one to spend eternity in. In the first room, people are standing in shit up to their necks. The guy says, 'No, let me see the next room.' In the second room, people are standing with shit up to their noses. The man says no again. Finally, Satan opens the door to the third room. People are standing with shit up to their knees, drinking coffee and eating Danish pastries. The guy says, 'I pick this room.' Satan says 'OK,' and starts to leave, and the guy wades in and starts pouring some coffee. On the way out, Satan yells, 'OK, coffee break's over. Everyone back on your heads!'

My grandfather always said, 'Don't watch your money; watch your health.' So one day while I was watching my health, someone stole my money. It was my grandfather.

A man joins a monastery and takes a vow of silence: he's allowed to say two words every seven years. After the first seven years, the elders bring him in and ask for his two words. 'Cold floors,' he says. They nod and send him away. Seven more years pass. They bring him back in and ask for his two words. He clears his throat and says, 'Bad food.' They nod and send him away. Seven more years pass. They bring him in for his two words. 'I quit,' he says. 'That's not surprising,' the elders say. 'You've done nothing but complain since you got here.'

They say animal behaviour can warn you when an earthquake is coming. Like the night before that last earthquake hit: our family dog took the car keys and drove to Arizona.

Two guys are walking down the street when a mugger approaches them and demands their money. They both grudgingly pull out their wallets and begin taking out their cash. Just then, one guy turns to the other and hands him a note. 'Here's that £20 I owe you,' he says.

I was walking across a bridge one day, and I saw a man standing on the edge, about to jump off. So I ran over and said, 'Stop! Don't do it!' 'Why shouldn't I?' he said. 'Well, there's so much to live for!' 'Like what?' 'Well ... are you religious?' He said yes. I said, 'Me too! Are you Christian or Buddhist?' 'Christian.' 'Me too! Are you Catholic or Protestant?' 'Protestant.' 'Me too! Are you

Episcopalian or Baptist?' 'Baptist.' 'Wow! Me too! Are you Baptist Church of God or Baptist Church of the Lord?' 'Baptist Church of God.' 'Me too! Are you original Baptist Church of God, or are you Reformed Baptist Church of God?' 'Reformed Baptist Church of God.' 'Me too! Are you Reformed Baptist Church of God, reformation of 1879, or Reformed Baptist Church of God, reformation of 1915?' He said, 'Reformed Baptist Church of God, reformation of 1915!' I said, 'Die, heretic scum!', and pushed him off.

I always look for a woman who has a tattoo. I see a woman with a tattoo, and I'm thinking, OK, here's a gal who's capable of making a decision she'll regret in the future.

A guy shows up late for work. The boss yells 'You should have been here at 8.30!' He replies, 'Why? What happened at 8.30?'

A Jewish man is walking on the beach when he discovers a bottle containing genie. He rubs it and a genie comes out, promises to grant him one wish. He says, 'Peace in the Middle East, that's my wish.' The genie looks concerned, then says, 'No, I'm sorry, that's just not possible. Some things just can't be changed. Do you have another wish?' The guy says, 'Well … for my whole life I've never received oral sex from my wife. That would be my wish.' The genie pauses for another moment and then says, 'How would you define peace?'

I can't think of anything worse after a night of drinking than waking up next to someone and not being able to remember their name, or how you met, or why they're dead.

Saul is working in his store when he hears a booming voice from above: 'Saul, sell your business.' He ignores it. It goes on for days. 'Saul, sell your business for $3 million.' After weeks of this, he relents and sells his store. The voice says, 'Saul, go to Las Vegas.' He asks why. 'Saul, take the $3 million to Las Vegas.' He obeys, goes to a casino. The voice says, 'Saul, go to the blackjack table and put it down all on one hand.' He hesitates, but knows he must. He's dealt an eighteen. The dealer has a six showing. 'Saul, take a card.' 'What? The dealer has...' 'Take a card!' He tells the dealer to hit him. Saul gets an ace. Nineteen. He breathes easy. 'Saul, take another card.' What? 'TAKE ANOTHER CARD!' He asks for another card. It's another ace. He has twenty. 'Saul, take another card,' the voice commands. 'I have twenty!' Saul shouts. 'TAKE ANOTHER CARD!' booms the voice. 'Hit me,' Saul says. He gets another ace. Twenty-one. The booming voice goes, 'Un-fucking-believable!'

TV adverts now show you how detergents take out bloodstains, a pretty violent image there. I think if you've got a T-shirt with a bloodstain all over it, maybe laundry isn't your biggest problem.

My sister was with two men in one night. She could hardly walk after that. Can you imagine? Two dinners!

A father is explaining ethics to his son, who is about to go into business. 'Suppose a woman comes in and orders a hundred dollars' worth of material. You wrap it up, and you give it to her. She pays you with a $100 bill. But as she goes out the door you realise she's given you two $100 bills. Now, here's where the ethics come in: should you or should you not tell your partner?'

A Jewish guy goes into a confession box. 'Father O'Malley,' he says, 'my name is Emil Cohen. I'm seventy-eight years old. Believe it or not, I'm currently involved with a 28-year-old girl, and also, on the side, her nineteen-year-old sister. We engage in all manner of pleasure, and in my entire life I've never felt better.' 'My good man,' says the priest, 'I think you've come to the wrong place. Why are you telling me?' And the guy goes, 'I'm telling everybody!'

I was on the Tube, sitting on a newspaper, and a guy comes over and asks, 'Are you reading that?' I didn't know what to say. So I said yes. I stood up, turned the page, and sat down again.

Last night I went to a 24-hour shop. When I got there, the guy was locking the front door. I said, 'Hey, the sign says you're open 24 hours.' He goes, 'Not in a row!'

Two Irishmen are fishing. One of them reels in his line and sees that he's snagged an old bottle. As he's taking it off the hook, a genie pops out and promises to grant him one wish. 'Turn the lake into beer,' he says. The genie goes 'Poof!' and the lake turns into beer. The man turns to his friend: 'So, what do you think?' His friend says, 'You idiot. Now we've got to piss in the boat.'

I failed my driver's test. The guy asked me 'What do you do at a red light?' I said, 'I don't know … look around, listen to the radio.'

Sid and Irv are business partners. They make a deal that whichever one dies first will contact the living one from the afterlife. So Irv dies. Sid doesn't hear from him for about a year, and figures there is no afterlife. Then one day he gets a call. It's Irv. 'So there is an afterlife! What's it like?' Sid asks. 'Well, I sleep very late. I get up, have a big breakfast. Then I have sex, lots of sex. Then I go back to sleep, but I get up for lunch, have a big lunch. Have some more sex. Take a nap. Huge dinner. More sex. Go to sleep, and wake up the next day.' 'Oh my God,' says Sid. 'So that's what heaven is like?' 'Oh no,' says Irv. 'I'm not in heaven. I'm a bear in Yellowstone Park.'

A man tells his psychiatrist, 'It was terrible. I was away on business, and I emailed my wife to say I'd be back a day early. I rushed home from the airport and found her in bed with my best friend. I don't get it. How could she do this to me?' 'Well,' says the psychiatrist. 'Maybe she didn't see the email.'

An old woman goes to view her husband's body before the funeral and becomes very upset. 'You have him in a brown suit and I wanted him in a blue suit.' The mortician says, 'We'll take care of it, ma'am,' and yells back, 'Ed, switch the heads on two and four!'

Stuffed deer heads on walls are bad enough, but it's worse when you see them wearing dark glasses, having streamers around their necks and a hat on their antlers. Because then you know they were enjoying themselves at a party when they were shot.

A man is driving his five-year-old to a friend's house when another car races in front and cuts them off, nearly causing an accident. 'Douchebag!' the father yells. A moment later he realises the indiscretion, pulls over and turns to face his son. 'Your father just said a bad word,' he says. 'I was angry at that driver, but that was no excuse for what I said. It was wrong. But just because I said it, it doesn't make it right, and I don't ever want to hear you saying it. Is that clear?' His son looks at him and says, 'Too late, douchebag.'

A guy asks a lawyer what his fee is. 'I charge £50 for three questions,' the lawyer says. 'That's awfully steep, isn't it?' the guy asks. 'Yes,' the lawyer replies. 'Now what's your final question?'

I went to a fight the other night and a hockey game broke out.

A Catholic teenager goes to confession, and after confessing to an affair with a girl is told by the priest that he can't be forgiven unless he reveals who the girl is. 'I promised not to tell!' he says. 'Was it Mary Patricia, the butcher's daughter?' the priest asks. 'No, and I said I wouldn't tell.' 'Was it Mary Elizabeth, the printer's daughter?' 'No, and I still won't tell!' 'Was it Mary Francis, the baker's daughter?' 'No,' says the boy. 'Well, son,' says the priest, 'I have no choice but to excommunicate you for six months.' Outside, the boy's friends ask what happened. 'Well,' he says, 'I got six months, but three good leads.'

There's always one of my uncles who watches a boxing match with me and says, 'Sure. Ten million pounds. You know, for that kind of money, I'd fight him.' As if someone is going to pay £200 a ticket to see a 57-year-old carpet salesman get hit in the face once and cry.

I knew these Siamese twins. They moved to America so the other one could drive.

I was making love to this girl and she started crying. I said, 'Are you going to hate yourself in the morning?' She said, 'No. I hate myself now.'

The guy who shot Robert Kennedy, Sirhan Sirhan, goes up for parole every year. Once he even told the parole board that if Kennedy was alive today, he would speak in his favour and tell them to let him go. What a tough break, you know? The one guy who would have supported him, and he shot him.

A man goes to a psychiatrist and says, 'Doc, my brother's crazy, he thinks he's a chicken.' The doctor says, 'Why don't you turn him in?' The guy says, 'We would. But we need the eggs.'

New York now leads the world's great cities in the number of people around whom you shouldn't make a sudden move.

Sincerity is everything. If you can fake that, you've got it made.

A lawyer dies and goes to heaven. 'There must be some mistake,' the lawyer argues. 'I'm too young to die. I'm only fifty-five.' 'Fifty-five?' says St Peter. 'No, according to our calculations, you're eighty-two.' 'How'd you get that?' the lawyer asks. Answers St Peter: 'We added up your time sheets.'

I went to my doctor and told him, 'My penis is burning.' He said, 'That means somebody is talking about it.'

If this is coffee, please bring me some tea. If this is tea, please bring me some coffee.

Last night, it was so cold the flashers were only describing themselves.

At the airport they asked me if anybody I didn't know gave me anything. Even the people I know don't give me anything.

I want to have children, but my friends scare me. One of my friends told me she was in labour for thirty-six hours. I don't even want to do anything that feels good for thirty-six hours.

Two ministers doing missionary work in the South Seas are captured by a tribe and tied to stakes. The chief says to them, 'You have a choice – death, or ugga bugga.' The first guy says, 'Well, I guess ugga bugga.' The chief shouts 'UGGA BUGGA!' and thirty members of the tribe attack and sodomise the first missionary. The chief then asks the second minister, 'Now you have a choice, death or ugga bugga.' He says, 'Well, my religion does not allow me to choose ugga bugga, so I suppose it must be death.' The chief says, 'Very well,' and shouts 'DEATH. But first, UGGA BUGGA!'

Three comedians are shooting the breeze at the back of a nightclub after a late gig. They've heard one another's material so much, they've reached the point where they don't need to say the jokes any more to amuse each other – they just need to refer to each joke by a number. 'Number 37!' cracks the first comic, and the others break up. 'Number 53!' says the second guy, and they howl. Finally, it's the third comic's turn. '44!' he quips. He gets nothing. 'What?' he asks. 'Isn't 44 funny?' 'Sure, it's usually hilarious,' they answer. 'But the way you tell it…'

I always keep a supply of stimulant handy in case I see a snake, which I also keep handy.

A man has a parrot that can sing and speak beautifully. He takes it to the synagogue on Rosh Hashanah and makes a wager that the bird can conduct the High Holiday service better than the temple's cantor. When the big moment comes, though, the parrot is silent. The guy is outraged. He takes the bird home and is about to kill it when the bird finally speaks: 'Schmuck! Think of the odds we'll get on Yom Kippur!'

When I went to college, my parents threw a going-away party for me, according to their letter.

A car hits a Jewish man. The paramedic rushes over and says, 'Are you comfortable?' The guy says, 'I make a good living.'

My grandfather is hard of hearing. He needs to read lips. I don't mind him reading lips, but he uses one of those yellow highlighters.

Waiters and waitresses are becoming nicer and much more caring. It used to be that I'd pay my cheque and they'd say 'Thank you.' That graduated into 'Have a nice day.' That's now escalated into 'You take care of yourself, now.' The other day I paid my cheque – the waiter said, 'Don't put off that mammogram.'

A comedian is sitting at the bar of a comedy club late one night when a beautiful woman comes up to him and says, 'I saw you perform tonight, and you're the funniest guy I've ever seen. I want to take you home and give you the hottest night of sex you've ever had.' The comedian looks at her and says, 'Did you see the first show or the second show?'

Two old actors are sitting on a bench. One says, 'How long has it been since you had a job?' The other actor says, 'Thirty-two years – how about you?' The first actor says, 'That's nothing. I haven't had a job in forty years!' The other says, 'One of these days we've got to get out of this business!'

My wife and I took out life insurance policies on each other – so now it's just a waiting game.